S0-AAZ-670

Additional commentary on

SEVEN PATHS TO POVERTY

"Very productive insights in a candid, simple format. Parents will clamor to pass this information on to the kids. Vital messages on the marketer's unrelenting attack on your wallet." – *Larry Nelson, Principal, Davis Partners LLC*

"I read *Seven Paths to Poverty* on the plane—couldn't put it down. Congratulations to Byrne and Mason. This should be on every college grad's gift list!" -- *Chuck Wilke, President, Managing Director, Meridian Capital LLC, Seattle, Washington*

"In simple, short, and entertaining doses, Drs. Mason and Byrne champion the enduring power of compound interest and the achievement of financial freedom with less, not more, risk. A delight to read." – *Edward J. McKinley, Private Equity Advisor to investment managers and institutions*

"I like it! The wisdom in *Seven Paths* reminds me of the beneficial advice from Richard McKenzie's *Getting Rich In America*, a book I gave to my students. Good stuff -- should be made readily available to high school kids." – *Ron Mittino, High School and Work Experience Teacher*

"This book provides common-sense building blocks for constructing a solid financial future. There's no 'magic bullet' for monetary security, but Byrne and Mason lay out the steps that are so often overlooked." – *C. Douglas Ades, Advisor on International Economic Development, Director FM Bank, Warsaw, Poland*

"While *Seven Paths* is addressed to Young America, its thesis is equally valid to the estimated 2.5 billion people in the world who lack access to everyday banking finance." – *Robin McPhail, Emerging Markets Group, London, UK*

"An original! *Seven Paths to Poverty* will shake up your spending patterns and alert you to hidden 'money traps.' Thousands of books promise instant wealth but few offer this book's risk-free strategies to find the capital that underpins long-tern security." – *Robert B. Tucker, President, Innovation Resource Consulting Group, author of* Innovation Is Everybody's Business

"A wise man said, 'If you save part of everything you earn, you'll never be broke.' This is a great refresher course on that philosophy for all adults, a "must read" for every young person." -- *William Campbell, Tennis Director, Sacramento State University, and Margie Campbell, Northern California Tennis Hall of Fame,*

SEVEN PATHS
TO
POVERTY

$ $ $

Finding Financial Stability
In an Unstable World

Gary Byrne, PhD
Lance Mason, DDS

☙ Newcastle & Knowles, Book Publishers ☙
Auckland – Madrid – New York – Santa Barbara
www.sevenpathstopoverty.com

Original paperback edition published in 2010 by Newcastle & Knowles, Book Publishers.

SEVEN PATHS TO POVERTY. Copyright © 2010 by Gary Byrne and Lance Mason, Newcastle & Knowles. All rights reserved; copying, reproducing, or transmitting this publication, in whole or in part, by any means, tangible or electronic, recording, information storage media, or by any other manipulation of intellectual property herein contained is specifically prohibited without the written permission of Newcastle & Knowles.

This publication is specifically intended for personal education, not financial advisory, purposes. Some names and settings are fictionalized for privacy and/or illustration purposes, but all material facts for the purposes of reader benefit are true to the best of the authors' knowledge. This book is not intended as a conduit for financial or investment advice, and is hereby specifically withheld from that role. The authors encourage the reader and all others to seek professional financial advice and guidance in the management of their financial affairs. The authors and publisher of this book accept no liability, risk, or loss incurred by others from the material herein contained.

PRINTED IN THE UNITED STATES OF AMERICA.

ISBN 978-0-615-37631-8

PLEASE VISIT:

www.sevenpathstopoverty.com

CONTENTS

Preface

PART I   OPENING THE MAP

PART II   THE SEVEN PATHS

PREFACE

The pivotal truth behind this book is that nearly all of us, between our teens and retirement, handle enough money to become actual millionaires. Even in hard times, a little bit of money flows through everyone's fingers, week by week, month by month. But small and large chunks of it get lost in the 24/7 "buy" message from the media and marketing industries. Carefully examined, how you use that money, even lesser amounts, and how you tie that use to your goals of future financial security and enjoyment of life are the things we hope to teach you here. It's not always easy, but it can be fun if you learn to enjoy it. And, like any good game, the more you do it, the better you get.

Many of us have faced, or are facing, financial distress, locked in a battle to rescue our material lives. In 2008-09, a decade-long investment flood ran dry and a lot of very smart people died of thirst as the Wall Street and real estate chiselers of the world bilked their trusting investors of billions. That's the bad news. The good news is that so many of us are or have been in the same boat. Why is that good news? Because it shows that you didn't get in trouble because you're naïve, stupid, or lazy. You don't create the massive economic factors that dictate trends on Wall Street, but the smaller business of your own life and finances are yours to control. It's not easy, but you can recover, and we're here to show you how, to save you from a bleak but avoidable financial washout. Why do so many people get hurt in really tough times? Because they don't know what we reveal in this book.

The Sunny Side

The inspiration for *Seven Paths* came to Gary Byrne one day on his bike. He and another professor cycled past a man panhandling and smoking. Neither Gary nor Richard smoke, but they have other addictions: monetary trends and human behavior. They asked each other, "What is the *capitalized value* of smoking?" That is, if the money spent today on smoking was invested instead, what could it be worth in the future?

That sounds complex, but it's not. Just add up a year's cost of cigarettes or any small daily or weekly purchase, say $5 a day ($35 a week; $1825 a year). Then pretend not to spend it, but to save and invest it at a certain interest rate for a certain period. If we start with $1825 at age twenty, and keep it invested until age sixty, what would be the outcome of this small act of *deferred gratification?* What IS the capitalized value of "small money" expenses?*

It's astounding to see how large this investment

*See Guidepost #1

grows over that time. So astounding, we think this discovery will change your views of money, value, saving, and wealth. Even though sensitive to these things, both Byrne and Mason were astonished by the answer – *almost $1 million!* This growth, this "wealth equation," based on a few dollars a week over long periods, and the downstream benefits, is the START button to your monetary goals, and a *critical crossroads* to your financial future.

The Evil Arrayed Against You

This sounds like common sense, to cut a few expenses. Why should that be difficult? Because common sense isn't that common. Because there are dark and powerful forces designed to separate you from your money at the first possible opportunity, to highjack your future security. Among the most pertinent revelations in this book are the myriad examples of how average people – us, you, your best friends, your co-workers – let the media, celebrities, passing trends, a moment's impulse, and other people's choices dictate our lives. We reveal how we are trained by marketers and merchandisers to ignore our values, our future, to ignore how we waste our hard-earned income on a thousand things we don't need. These habits and patterns, distortions of what we know inside to be good for us, are waiting to drag us to the poorhouse, through the bankruptcy courts, and through a life of constant financial fear.

An ignorance of history combined with the potential distortions caused by recent memory will put us in peril. The "prosperity and wealth" of the western world, as most of us perceive them, are less than a few decades old: most material possessions of today didn't exist fifty years ago; a huge fraction of today's technology is less than twenty years old. These "time warps" can deceive us in terms of what is enduring, what has underlying meaning, and what can be easily lost through personal miscalculation or the inevitable disruptions that our rapidly changing world creates. This "wealth" can be lost almost as fast as it's been gained unless we each plan carefully for our individual futures.

Ready For Take-Off

So, what you are reading is the downstream culmination of Gary Byrne's afternoon bike ride. This book will help you realize you were born with great financial security within simple reach. But you must leave a few unnecessary expenses behind, get on the road to security, and not be derailed by the "seven paths to poverty." You will be able to find honest meaning in the material world, and create a better, more independent life. This book is not about investing money, but about finding the money to invest by avoiding the most common ways to lose it.

All important journeys begin with the right preparation. So, at the outset, we provide you with two *guideposts,* verbal diagrams for the mental and psychological planning needed to get beneficial financial change. Then come the seven infamous paths, in which we explain the seven common avenues that lead most people into monetary hardship *AND* how to steer clear of them. Incorporating these lessons into your life's journey will lay the groundwork for your economic welfare.

While the timing and the lessons of the 2008-09 economic crisis have highlighted the benefits in *Seven Paths,* what we hope the book offers are timeless solutions that will continue to benefit the reader long after the wounds of any current hardships are healed.

We wish you freedom.

PART I

OPENING THE MAP

GUIDEPOST #1

How Do You Eat an Elephant?

Trying to tackle large problems is always intimidating. They always seem bigger than us. They *can* look like elephants, and we can feel like pygmies in the face of them. So, then, "How *do* you eat an elephant?" To answer this riddle we offer an old piece of pygmy wisdom: One bite at a time. Divide the problem up and conquer it one piece at a time.

Many people reading this book know they have financial problems, some of them large, perhaps even crippling. Grocery bills seem to enlarge while food on the table seems to shrink. Rent or a mortgage that was manageable last year now looks like the national debt. A much needed upgrading of your wardrobe, business premises, or home now seems out of reach. Family expenses may leave too little to enjoy a short vacation or, for a young person, it might be the simple weekly and monthly bills as he or she starts out in the world. Whatever this problem or combination of problems may be, we know they can look insurmountable.

Like the pygmy confronting an elephant, you have to cut big problems down to size. You have to divide them into manageable bits and "eat" them one small bit at a time. That is the fundamental design of this book. We divided the "bad habits" of monetary loss into seven basic pathways or patterns, patterns that lead even the willing person into financial distress. We analyzed what makes these pathways damaging, and designed strategies and tactics to work your way out of them and into a much more secure future.

The First Step

To explore the patterns in people's lives that have led many to financial hardship, we're going to take you on a journey. The starting point for this journey is the question "What motivates you?" Your reply will define how, today and throughout your life, you will read – and stick to – the "map" we present in this book. The question also explores three critical elements of the journey, major *road signs* along the way – *goals, values,* and *security*. These are small words but mammoth concepts, and essential to understanding life and making it a lasting success. But, as with any journey, a study of the terrain before you begin will give you a clearer perspective of the landscape and its challenges. That's the role of these first two chapters, to prepare you to absorb the tactics and strategies for navigating unharmed down the *Seven Paths to Poverty.*

Goals

Goals, in all shapes and sizes, conscious or unconscious, are behind every act we do, every choice we make. They are geared to *achieve* what we want and to *avoid* what we don't want. Education, the freedom to travel, good health, some new clothes – these are all *acquisition* goals, things you might want and will work for. Breaking a bad habit, reducing job stress, and evading poverty are *avoidance* goals, also worthwhile and also requiring courage and hard work. And we really like the third one, evading poverty, because it's the entire focus of this book.

Values

Our *values* reflect what we know to be true about ourselves, and how we use or ignore that knowledge in our decisions. Values provide critical directions on the road to happiness and contentment, so they need to be a big part of our choices. We'll talk a lot about personal values and how to understand them.

As a basic animal instinct, *security* is closely tied to goal-seeking. We all want security; we pursue it from birth and, in that sense, it's everybody's goal. It comes in different forms – physical, domestic, financial, emotional, health – and any journey that ignores security as a purpose will struggle for success.

Driving Forces

Goals, values, and security are major motivators

in our lives, great sources of direction on the journey you're about to take.   What about *MONEY?*   Sure, money's a legitimate motivator: it rewards us (satisfying goals and values) and protects us from harm (providing security).   These are among the most basic drives of all living things, and money fits there.   Let's look at some other signposts you'll encounter on the road.

Threat can be a motivator.   Injury and death are potholes in the road that create basic human fears.   In our *physical* lives, these threats are self-explanatory (a punch in the nose = injury; the guillotine = death).   But in our social, cultural, and economic lives, *injury* can sidetrack us in other ways (bigotry, poor education, financial hardship), while *death* can be symbolic (bankruptcy, homelessness) rather than actual.   In any event, we're motivated at a very basic level to avoid threats on the way to welfare and safety.

As we follow the map of our lives, we pursue goals that bring us *pleasure, promise,* and a *sense of belonging.*   Biologically, from birth, we seek out people and processes that *nurture* and *protect* us.   As we develop, we seek approval for our actions from others. We also generate a *sense of self,* images of how we see ourselves on our journey.   From them, we'll try to fulfill whichever images, or visions, we think are in our best interests.   These things reveal our *values* and reinforce our larger *goals.*

It's not our aim to write a book on the philosophy of human existence, so let's try to boil this down.   We have four motivations: to avoid *death,* to avoid *injury,* to gain *approval* from those we honor, and to *fulfill* our goals and the best images we have of ourselves. Nearly all human action is fueled by these four incentives. The first two are based on threats, and if you remove the threat you remove the motivation. If you force a person to act by holding a stick over him, that only works until you remove the stick, and you've done nothing for that person's self-esteem or reliability.

The second two motivations, outside approval and goal achievement, are "self-propagating": both give a positive reward plus higher self-esteem, spurring us to repeat the action. (For more on this, read Abraham Maslow's "A Theory of Human Motivation" and his Hierarchy of Needs. New research into endorphins' role explains how and why we get pleasure from achieving goals.) We'll use the truths about these behaviors to guide you along the highway to financial success, and imprint into <u>your</u> head the self-image of a traveler who's achieving goals now and in the future, holding to your values, and having fun doing it. While we can't turn you into that person – only you can do that – we will give you a map and a vehicle to take you from where you are to where you want to be, and teach you the skills to navigate the roads.

Keep in mind that you may encounter "elephants" along the route and will have to use what you learn here to "eat" them. *And* we're not above using poverty as a gentle threat to keep you on your toes, because threats do work, in some circumstances. It's from that truth that Gary Byrne derived the title for this book, and we include it in the chapters that deal with the pitfalls of unexamined spending.

Setting Goals

There's no question about the importance of *goal-setting* to achieve what you want in life. So how do you do it? How do you go from nowhere to somewhere? First, pick an aspect of your life that you would like to change, and that you feel you *need* to change. Decide on a concrete goal that would fulfill that change. That goal should connect to something you find admirable, fulfilling, or in some other way *valuable* to your life – family security, personal freedom, education, genuine self-esteem. Since this book is about money, good examples might be an investment nest-egg, saving for travel abroad, school expenses, the cost of a self-improvement venture.

Next, the goal has to be *"committable."* There can't be anything big in your life or in the nature of the goal that prevents you from committing to it. It can't be against your core beliefs in life, conflicting with your family life, illegal, damaging to others, and so on. Also it must be *achievable* – too high, you'll fail and be frustrated; too low, and it won't be worthwhile. Finally, *write the goal down* and keep that piece of paper or computer file. Why? Because a written goal is a contract with yourself.

Achieving

Now you have your goal or goals. What's next? Figure out a *method* to achieve the goal; write that down, too. This might just be self-discipline: your goal is saving $40 a week, and the method would be to stop buying some things you can do without, and sticking to that. But your goal may involve other people, a second job, a life-style change, or another activity with complexities that require more management. So, it's often important to create a *plan* to execute the *method* to achieve the *goal*. You and two friends need $30,000 to start a business venture, so you must find $10,000 each of investment capital. That requires more planning. Three steps, five steps, ten steps to the plan – it doesn't matter, but the more long-range or complex the method, or the more it involves others, or has a demanding set of moves to work out, then the more likely you need a plan to execute the method.

So the order of *goal-setting* is Goal → Method → Plan. The order of *execution* is Plan → Method → Goal. These simple formulas should help you get on the road.

Habits and Other Enemies

Habits are hard to change. Build up your commitment to yourself before you begin. Remember Oscar Wilde's words, "I can resist anything but temptation," and don't let yourself get defeated right out of the gate because of inadequate mental preparation. And don't procrastinate. *Start early. Start now.*

Forces of opposition are arrayed against you. Don't let them defeat you. The media will be constantly trying to undermine your goals, to distract you, to get you to

spend-spend-spend.   Deferring   your   gratification
requires some discipline and even courage. You are the
hero and they are the villains! Keep your white hat on.
Persevere! Freedom and security are waiting for you.

   CAUTION: there are many more money-traps out
there.   In Path One, we discuss the importance of
holding your power against the enemy, and in Path Two
we focus on the *Slow Leak,* the outflow of "small
money." Then, in the following chapters, we introduce
and explain many larger and more consequential ways to
keep control of your material welfare.

The Algebra of Pachyderms

   At the beginning of this chapter, we asked "How do
you eat an elephant?" and talked about attacking large
problems one bite at a time. Now let's turn the question
around – How do you *create* an elephant? How do you
create a large pool of capital for financial security?
Exactly the same way – one bite at a time, using small
amounts that build to big amounts. And what do you
start with? *Motivations and goals.* We are going to give
you the facts and figures so you can choose and set your
goals, but you have to provide the motivation. And this
is a *long-term* game, not a get-rich-quick scheme. If you
want that, go to Las Vegas. If you want to get the
benefits of this book, you've got to have short-term and
long-term discipline. It has to become a habit. But it's a
good habit, and it can be a fun habit if you look at it like
you're playing a game.

If there is a "secret" here to reaching your financial goals, it is hidden in the answer to the *wealth equation* we raised in the Preface: What will small amounts of money, invested consistently for a long time, be worth in the future? That secret is *compound interest.* This is a term familiar to some readers but Greek to others, so we're going to explain it. Compound interest (or its cousin, compound return) has been called a financial miracle, a banker's conjuring, a mysterious formula. It's not. It's just a tool that turns a little long-term discipline into a lot of money. How? Instead of spending an investment's earnings as they come in, you use that cash – all of it – to immediately buy more of the same investment, year after year. So every year's earnings add on to the original investment and create their own earnings, year after year, every year through the life of the investment, all *compounding* on top of themselves. (All references in the coming pages to earning interest will mean *compound interest.)*

First, let's start with a simple example of compound interest to show you how it works. You put $100 into an investment that pays you 10% interest per year, that is, $10. So, at the end of the year you'll have $110 (For those who think 10% is unrealistic, we justify it below.). If you spend the $10, you're back to $100, and at the end of the second year you'll have $110 again. Third year, the same. But if after the first year you leave the whole $110 in the investment, at the end of the second year you'll have $110 + 10% (i.e., $11) = $121 – the investment is *compounding;* the interest you reinvested is now earning its own interest.

Still, it doesn't sound much different, does it, $100, $110, $121? But after five years, you'd have $161 (instead of $110), after ten years, $260, and after twenty years, $680. If you did this from the time you were twenty until you were sixty, i.e. forty years, your $100 would become $5000. You only put in $100 of your own cash, and the rest of it grew from earning compound interest. And that's only from the *first* $100 you invested. What if you continued to invest $100 *every* year at 10%, and never took anything out until the end?

This part of the discussion is *absolutely critical.* Let's consider it a piece at a time. One investment of $100 for twenty years at 10% becomes $700. But $100 invested *every* year for twenty years at 10% grows to over *$6000*. $2000 in, more than $6000 out. Pretty darn good. But in the next twenty years the investment *really* explodes in value. Think of those first twenty years as the time it takes to reach "critical mass." Because over the second twenty years, $100 every year grows to $48,684. Over forty years, you invested a total of $4000 of your own cash, and you got nearly $50,000 at the other end, twelve times your money.

The Million Dollar Question

That $50,000 is worth saving for; but suppose that instead of $100 each year, you saved and invested a lot more, year after year? This brings us back to the math question we asked in the preface: How much does $5 a day become over the long term? Here's the answer:

Figure any target expense – convenience food or drink, grooming "extras," designer groceries, or, yes, cigarettes – at $5 a day for one year. That's $35 a week or $1825 for the year. If that money was not spent, but instead invested from age twenty to age sixty at 10% compounded interest, using the same math formula we use above, the result would be $85,000. Yes, *$85,000.00* – a big stack of money. $1825 in, $85,000 out. That's called the "capitalized value" of money: how much you would have earned from it over a certain period of time if you hadn't spent the money at the beginning, but invested it. Not bad – a *45-times* increase in your money.

But you know what? *Chicken feed!* That $85,000 only represents the return from *one year's* savings. If you did the same thing the next year at age twenty-one, that second $1825, invested for thirty-nine years, would be worth nearly $78,000. And so on. And so on. A year's money for cigarettes or mountain bike goodies or boutique cappuccinos, anything that adds up to $1825 a year, invested *every* year between the ages of twenty and sixty would total over <u>$900,000</u> (See P. 16, Table I). Yes, almost *one million dollars* – that's what it costs you for every $5 a day you *don't* save and invest each year. It's *never* too late to start, but try to start early. And don't spend it until you're rich.

We know that a lot of you are over twenty; we'll talk about that later, too. And a lot of you don't want to wait until you're sixty to have financial fun, to which we have two responses: first, we'll show you how to do it (somewhat) sooner; second, sixty gets here a lot faster than you think. So be ready.

Them's Fightin' Words

Some people will dispute 10% returns as being unrealistically high, but Gary Byrne did the research. The compounded annual return on the stock market over *sixty years,* from 1948 to 2008, was over 12%. Stocks rose in value an average of 7.3% per year, with an average cash dividend of 4.7%. So, on average, if you bought a stock during this time for $10, that stock would have been worth $10.73 a year later, and would have paid you $0.47 in cash over that year.   For a compounded return, you would put the $0.47 into the stock, meaning you would own $11.20 worth of stock at the beginning of the second year ($10.73 + .47 = $11.20). And you would keep doing that every year. (While stocks can take big hits at times, they have never failed to return to health.)

NOTE: these are only *illustrations.* If you invested for only one year, chances are huge you would get far less or far more. These figures are *averages* over sixty years. You have to be in the market for many years for your investment to mirror long-term market averages. *And* no one knows what the stock market will do over the next sixty years. Or even five. But Gary's study shows a compound return of 12%+ since 1948. So, for the sake of most of our discussion, we're going to stay with 10%. We will be writing extensively on investment concepts and strategies in our next book, *The Seven Golden Doors.*

NOTE: "compound return" versus "compound interest," and variations from 10%. Talking about *compound interest* (C.I.) on investments usually assumes the *interest is the only return* on the investment. For instance, a bond just pays out interest as cash. To *compound* the interest, you buy more of the same bonds with that cash as it comes in. But, unlike a bond, stock and real estate may go up in value *and* deliver other returns, as well. These other returns, often termed distributions, can be in the form of depreciation, capital gains, dividends, interest, and return of capital. So, when calculating *compound returns* (C.R.), we will include all these wealth increases as well as the investment's price increase, and assume that all cash distributions are cycled back into the same investment, i.e. not spent.

To illustrate some variations, Table II (P. 16) begins with an investment of $1000 and shows the growth of dollars across a range of compounded returns and various investment periods, while Table III (P. 16) shows compounded dollar returns from combining a range of dividend payouts with 10% growth from all other factors, where all cash distributions are put back into the investment. Returns of 15-20% are not realistic over a long term, but these illustrations do show the extreme power of compounding.

These details are important, but they can miss the BIG point – save and invest, using good investment advice and the necessary research, and you will be setting yourself up for life.

TABLE I

Number of Years	Beginning Total	Annual Addition	Year End Total
1	0	1,825	1,825
5	8,528	1,825	11,246
10	25,279	1,825	29,751
20	98,182	1,825	110,288
40	829,772	1,825	918,485

TABLE II

Number of Years	Capital Growth from Various Compounded Rates of Return				
	8%	10%	12%	15%	20%
1	1,080	1,100	1,120	1,150	1,200
5	1,469	1,611	1,762	2,011	2,488
10	2,159	2,594	3,106	4,046	6,192
20	4,661	6,727	9,646	16,367	38,338
40	21,725	45,259	93,051	267,864	1,469,772

TABLE III

Number of Years	Compounded Return from Various Dividends plus 10% Additional Growth				
	1%	2%	3%	5%	7%
1	1,110	1,120	1,130	1,150	1,170
5	1,685	1,762	1,842	2,011	2,192
10	2,839	3,106	3,395	4,046	4,807
20	8,062	9,646	11,523	16,367	23,106
40	65,001	93,051	132,782	267,864	533,869

An Essential Truth

As we said, this arithmetic applies no matter where the dollars come from. It can be money you spend on fashion, impulse, a habit, peer pressure, or simply the few bucks that go out without your thinking about it. To build a small fortune, to "create the elephant," you just need to find a little money to squirrel away each week, each month, each year for forty years – or twenty years, or ten years – it's never too late to start building security. You think you can't find enough from somewhere? We think you can, and we'll explain why and how. Just cut out a few small expenses that you can do without, and you can step off the paths to poverty. In fact, you can be rich. And we're not kidding. But it will take some work and some diligence—on the savings side, a wagon we push in this book, and on the investing side, which we'll study in our next book.

By the way, "capitalized value" is a very longstanding concept, and Byrne and Mason weren't the first to write about it in a book. But if this is the first time you've come across it, we hope you get it because it can serve as the main engine of your wealth machine, the rudder for your voyage out of financial storms and into profitable channels.

GUIDEPOST #2

Inner Power – Its Role in Financial Independence

The empires of the future will be empires of the mind –
Winston Churchill

How many people have you known or can you recall
from history who had power, real power, because
someone gave it to them? Napoleon didn't command
the Grand Army that conquered Europe because
someone handed him power, or because some Parisian
bread bakers thought he was cool, or because the King
of France thought Napoleon was entitled to power since
he was a short guy and deserved something he couldn't
get for himself. No. He had the power because *he felt it
in himself.* He set goals, won some battles, took the
power he got, focused on it, multiplied it, and then used
all he could muster to take control of most of Europe.

Good, bad, or ugly, the fact is that people who take
power over their own lives do so because they have
visions for themselves. They have dreams and
commitment. They set goals, and they use the power

they have, or the power they learn to develop, to pursue and achieve those goals. People talk nowadays about "empowerment." We're not sure, but we think that means trying to give power to people who either don't have it or don't know they have it, and who somebody else thinks ought to have it. It seems to us a contradiction in terms.

You can give someone help, and you can give him or her opportunities, but we don't believe you can give someone true power. Power is something a person has to find and take for himself, and it comes mainly from within. That doesn't mean powerful people are perfect, far from it. Nobody said Napoleon was a saint (not even the French). Some of the most powerful people in the world are the most twisted – like the man said, power corrupts, and absolute power corrupts absolutely. But that's *absolute* power, tremendous power over the lives of others, and that's not what we're talking about. We're talking about *inner* power over your own life, and, when necessary, over yourself. And *giving up the power over your own life* is certainly one path to poverty.

Where Power Resides

Power comes up time and again in debates about wealth and poverty. In his book *Powershift,* the great futurist Alvin Toffler talks about the sources and symbols of power. He describes three sources of power: physical power, wealth, and knowledge. We see these forms of power all around us today, back through history, and into the future. Force – guns and armies exert power and control. Riches – billions of dollars can make almost anything happen. Knowledge – information can bring success, move armies, create a fortune, or wipe it out. These have been well-recognized over time and across cultures – in the East and in the West – as instruments of power.

Toffler argues that knowledge is the most democratic of the three forms. Two different people can't wield the same weapon or control the same army. Two different companies can't make or invest the same dollar. But you and I can both possess the same information and use it at the same time. And the person who uses that knowledge best gets the most advantage. Even in warfare or in the art and science of finance, information is the most powerful element: strategy, tactics, espionage, weather, surprise – all knowledge-based forces that give power to the one who has the information first and uses it best.

The symbols of power in Japanese culture are a sapphire (wealth), a sword (physical might), and a mirror (wisdom, knowledge). The first two symbols are obvious, but what does the mirror mean? According to Toffler, the mirror symbolizes *self-* knowledge, the most powerful of all. If you can see yourself, *really* see yourself – your strengths, your flaws, your values – you have a power in life that few people do. It's a power that can understand and control all the other powers inside you.

But how many of us are going to command armies or have millions or billions to throw around, controlling the world's events? Very few. But the one thing everyone has access to is oneself. Looking inside ourselves, seeing what makes us tick as individuals, developing that information and that understanding, and the *power* that knowledge gives us to direct and control our lives – that is a power everyone has. There are few things as powerful in this world as a person with a genuine grasp of who he or she is, and the motivation to do something with it. We can't give you that power, but we can tell you where to look for it, and we can tell you how to use some of it to control the financial side of your life.

How Power Is Claimed

So why do we think power is so important? Because we're trying to start a cult devoted to mirror worship? No. It's because people often lose control of their financial lives because they lack *belief in themselves,* and that causes them to lack power. They don't believe there is anything they can do to get out, or stay out, of poverty. We want them to understand that they can not only stay out of poverty but *make themselves wealthy.* And the power to do that is inside them – inside *you.*

The power we're talking about is <u>will</u>power, the power to control the choices you make. This kind of power seems to have become a dirty word in an age when the advertisers feed us a daily diet of "The Life of Luxury We All Deserve," and we're surrounded by images of comfort and ease, everything available by credit card or monthly payments or home equity loans (the sub-prime cesspool has stunk up some of this). We are taught, from age five to eighty-five, from shampoo to SUVs, that we "deserve" the lavish lifestyle, or at least something close to it, and that we're failing if we don't have it. *Not true.* We deserve what our power can bring us, and *nothing more.*

There is a simple story, a true story, that seems to tie a lot of this together. In 1975, H.L. Hunt was thought by many to be the world's richest man. Opinions differ about how he got his start (inheritance, cotton farming, or draw poker), but they all agree on how he made it big – oil. Texas oil. He was rich at a time when a *billion dollars* really meant something. Serious dough. He was being interviewed by a writer, and it went something like this:

> *WRITER: Mr. Hunt, in 1930, you were a bankrupt cotton farmer in Arkansas, and now some say you're the richest man in the world. What was your secret to turning your life around, to rising out of poverty and controlling the largest fortune in America?*
>
> *HUNT: Ain't no secret, son, jest life. Fact is, only two things you gotta decide in this world. Furst one is whatcha want, 'n the second one is whatcha's prepared to pay to git it. An' the hardest one* (he might, at this point, have spit a stream of tobacco juice into some handy receptacle) *is th' furst one.*

What's the lesson here? It's that there's a price to pay for everything you want. No one's *entitled* to life's material comforts (though being born brilliant, lucky, or gorgeous puts you near the head of the line). No one *deserves* luxury carpet, a new motorcycle, or weekly visits to the nail salon. In this reality, you don't get what you deserve; you get what you negotiate. And most of that negotiating is *between you and yourself* – setting goals, planning how to achieve them, sticking to that vision, or failing to. (By the way, the best way to ruin any negotiation is by lying, so don't lie to yourself.)

But Mr. Hunt delivered an even deeper message – that before you decide what price you're prepared to pay, you need to decide *what* it is you want. And this is, as he says, the tough part. Why? Because to know what you truly want, what really is going to mesh with your *values,* make you *happy,* and give you lasting *satisfaction* once you have it (after all the *willpower* you're going to apply, right?), you have to learn the lesson of the Japanese mirror. You have to understand yourself. With that knowledge comes power, the power to choose, and choose wisely, where you will take your life.

Power, Biology, and Your Brain

There is important new research that gives a logical, biologic basis for much of what we're presenting here. The field is called neuroeconomics, and it is the study of how we think about money, rewards, goals, and so forth. Simply stated, there are corners of the brain that do the analytical stuff, and corners that do the emotional stuff. These things don't happen in the same places in the brain.

For example, we can *analyze* the logical arguments about spending $100 on a new sweater: cold weather is coming; I have three sweaters already; this one's on sale; it matches my eyes; there's no parking near the shop; I've got big expenses this month, and so on. But *emotional* forces flood in: I'm afraid to get more in debt; it looks *great* with my eyes; I may never see such a sweater again; my wife will *kill* me if I spend another $100.

The first set of thoughts run through the <u>cortex</u> of the brain; the second set through the <u>amygdala</u> and perhaps the <u>limbic</u> system. If the uncertainty of the outcome is strong enough and carries enough threat, the amygdala will send fear messages to the cortex and elsewhere to suppress the choice. If the pleasure-seeking parts of the brain can counteract the amygdala, and the cortex accepts the logic of the arguments, I might own the sweater by lunchtime but wait until the gun shops close before showing it to my wife.

Decision-making is a balance of power between what we think and how we feel, a truly mind-boggling mixture of electrical signals and brain chemicals (like endorphins) slapping each other around in a logic-based – but sometimes chaotic-feeling – series of encounters until, in a matter of days or perhaps milliseconds, I act out the decision, a decision that may be to accept a choice or reject a choice, depending on whether fear, pleasure, logic, reason, experience, enthusiasm, greed, or some combination of them wins out.

But one fact seems irrefutable: no action is ever taken on logic and analysis alone. You can apply reason until the cows come home; but, in what a golfing friend calls "paralysis by analysis," nothing will happen unless the actor experiences an emotional conviction for the choice. Emotion, positive or negative, must always emerge to force a decision into motion. Commitment to that decision is mostly an emotional step: though you can analyze your way to seeing all the benefits of a choice, you can't analyze your way into a commitment to that choice. That has to come from your enthusiasm for receiving those benefits – or avoiding some threats. (In most cases, this applies only to "active" choices, or choices that require something to change; if a decision is made to do nothing, to change nothing, then emotion may or may not be significant in that.)

The reason this is critical for you is that it explains the biological principles that can help you achieve your goals. Knowing how the decision-making mechanisms of your brain operate gives you more control over those functions. Knowing that choosing to spend *or* choosing to save both require combinations of analysis and emotion makes it clearer that they are both a choice. This is why we keep repeating "Think!" If you choose your goals, if you want to commit to them, then THINK about money choices when they come up. Think about the good sides and bad sides. Put in a little analysis – just a little.

Give the emotional side of your brain a chance to recognize the benefits of saving, of how that will keep you on track toward your goals. Resisting temptation will be seen as resisting weakness, as achieving, and lead to gratification. Your amygdala will cooperate, your endorphins will respond to the goal-oriented choice, and you will be more likely more often to make the choices this book – and your future – are designed around.

Nitty Gritty - The Unromantic Truth

Now you have the important tools to begin working your way out of your financial problems and putting down the groundwork for a secure future: setting and pursuing goals, finding the power and discipline inside yourself to achieve them, and an understanding of compound interest when you are ready to invest. But what do you do with these tools? How do you use them? The same way you eat the elephant: one bite at a time. So, what's the first bite? How do you start consuming this animal of financial fear?

By saving money.

Yes, saving money. Look, we admit it doesn't sound very sexy. We knew you might feel this way when we started writing the book. But remember the elephant. Finding "small bites" in your life, small things (and some big things) not to spend money on, is where you begin your monetary resurrection. Why did someone once say, "A penny saved is a penny earned?" Because it's true. Which is easier, to have $100 by not spending it, or to go out and earn it? Remember, to get a $100 from earning it, you have to earn $130 to $150 or more, depending on your tax bracket. And you actually have to *do* the additional work to earn it.

If there is one big message about how to save money, it's this: <u>Don't</u> <u>stop</u> <u>thinking</u> about how you spend your money. Don't step away from the decision. Don't give up your power. If you think, "Yes, I really want this or need this," fine. No argument. But be in the driver's seat. Don't let others control your choices.

Sure, there are more exciting ways to become millionaires. We know a guy who really *did* build a better mousetrap. Bob Noe invented The Rat Zapper, an "electric chair" for rats and mice, it's made him millions, and now, as Andrew Tobias says,* "He's getting all the girls." We know a maverick-minded, motorcycle-racing, creative-genius physics professor who became a so-called "titan of industry" and very rich besides. We know any number of self-made squillionaires. Inventors, investors, and inveterate schemers. Butchers (Farmer John), bakers (Sara Lee), candle-stick makers (Oneida) that churn out mega-bucks. Sometimes it seems that there are more people than fleas on a hound dog who have thought up new and incredible ways to turn ideas into chunks of cash so huge you couldn't lift them on your best day. They're called entrepreneurs. But you know what? Half the people in America who are broke are entrepreneurs who

* *In* The Only Investment Guide You'll Ever Need, *a wonderful book you* must *read.*

didn't make it.

Okay, that last sentence was an exaggeration. But take it from us: there is no *hidden secret* to getting rich.

Yes, there are some secrets to *being* rich, like being born in a Park Avenue mansion or into the Kuwaiti royal family. Or being born smart, lucky, and beautiful. But no one's luck runs forever, and it can go against you just when you've laid that big bet on the next card off the deck – or the next rally on Wall Street. As for being born beautiful, there are tens of thousands of almost-cover girls and boys trying to live off their looks on the highways and byways of The Big City, and regretting it. (Take it from us. We were beautiful once.)

And let's be honest. Most of us aren't Bill Gates – or even a Bob Noe. If we were, we'd be gluing transistors together in our garage, inventing "the next big thing," or poring over reports on the suppression of household vermin. The fact is that we aren't all financial wonks or real estate geniuses or investors with the Midas touch. And you *have a life.* But you just want it to be better and more secure, free from the fear that you're going to end up sleeping (with your spouse and kids?) under a railroad bridge. Yes, we've *all* felt *that* shiver down our spines at one time or another.

No, there are no magic formulas to acquiring wealth. Over thousands of years and millions of schemes, and the efforts and dreams of billions of people, that secret would be out by now. But, for average people like us, there is one sure way to *build* a fortune, to "create the elephant," and that is to save money and invest it carefully. We'll talk about this – a lot.

The View from Here

Wait! There is one secret to riches, and we explained it above – compound interest. And it's not really a secret, it just seems that way because of the way it sneaks up on you. It's a simple thing, but one that most people don't pay attention to, so it's not easy to grasp its power. It really is simple: invest some money in a compounding investment and just plow all the earnings back into the same investment. Then, many years later, about the time you almost forgot about it, it's worth . . . well, a lot.

Now we've told you the boring and horrible truth that, in order to use this secret, you have to save money. So it's time to start showing you all sorts of ways to do that.

Keep in mind, you've got friends who will ignore all this "saving money" malarkey, ignore their future security, and learn the seven paths to poverty the hard way. But not you. Your destination is a comfortable financial future – or more. To reach that goal, you need something to move you and keep you moving. That's why *power*, especially *willpower*, is so important. Call it discipline, call it inner strength, call it whatever you want – it's the force inside you that propels you along, that keeps you from running out of steam, from grinding to a halt. Your goals and direction will give you vision and enthusiasm for where you're going, and then the power you'll find *inside yourself* will push you and pull you up the road to great good fortune.

(The authors don't endorse particular products, but for the computer-literate reader there are a few popular programs that can help you reach your savings goals. One free one with a good reputation is www.mint.com, started by Aaron Patzer and recently acquired by Intuit, the company that owns Quicken. A web search will turn up many others.)

PART II

THE SEVEN PATHS

PATH ONE

Abandonment of Power

Financial torment is the end result for the person who gives up power to the relentless attacks of media, merchandising, and marketing.

The surrender of the personal power we analyzed in Guide Post #2 is the focus of this chapter. Of the seven paths to financial failure, this is probably the broadest and most direct, and a basic ingredient of the other six. Remember from G. P. #1 and #2: goal-setting plus personal power will lead you into the realm of wealth. Once you have a focus, goals are not hard to set; pursuing them through the exertion of personal power is. It requires real commitment, perseverance, and discipline. Surrendering your inner power means bailing out on your goals, bailing out on yourself.

A Brief History of Foolishness

Without getting messy and teary-eyed, let's look at some celebrated pieces of advice from across the spectrum of history and ethics:

- In his 19th Century poem "Invictus," represented recently in a film of the same name, William Ernest Henley said,

    "I am the master of my fate,
    I am the captain of my soul."

- Socrates told us in the 5th Century, B.C., *The unexamined life is not worth living.*

- *A fool and his money are soon parted* is attributed to a 16th Cent. sage, Thomas Tusser.

- And, finally, if you believe the legend, P.T. Barnum, the infamous showman and circus mogul of the 1900s, proclaimed, "There's a sucker born every minute."

Why have these renowned sayings survived and become recognized over the centuries? Because they are accurate reflections of human behavior. Because Socrates, Tusser, et al. didn't invent their observations, but simply reported what was known about human conduct back through history.

The timeless importance of the *power to decide and choose* lives on in these bits of wisdom, each with its own perspective. Henley tells us that we all pilot our own lives, steering onto the rocks or into clear water, under our own power. Socrates teaches that we must question ourselves and our choices, testing them for truth and legitimacy, proving and re-proving our viewpoints over time. Tusser pulls us into the world of commerce with a sharp thrust at mental laziness about money: If you act the fool with your spending power, you will soon be broke.

The remark attributed to Barnum puts a new and meaningful accent on the entire topic of choice and spending. Unlike Henley's captain or Tusser's fool, where strength or shortcomings *within the buyer* are the focus, P.T. exposes the subject of trickery—*external forces* that lay traps for the buyer, probe his ignorance, and exploit his naïveté. This is historically timely, because Barnum operated in the early years of advertising, when the media were learning how to sell space in the "information delivery systems" of the time (newspapers, magazines, building posters) to the merchandisers. Barnum, king-of-spin and profit-monger, grabbed any chance to turn the would-be consumer into a "sucker," and if clever and creative advertising was the way, he was agreeable.

A fool, a sucker, an incompetent captain, and an unexamined life--they all lack that same thing: *accurate information.* These four wise men from the past recognized the importance of information as a source of power.

St. Peter and the Salesman

In addition to famous sayings, a number of stories, some sincere and some blackly humorous, show the role of decision-making power.

Dave, the owner of a hardware store is killed in a car crash. Greeted by St. Peter at the gates of Heaven,

Dave's told he must relate the story of his life, after which, if he appears worthy, he'll be granted one wish and entry into Heaven. The tale Dave tells is of an honest merchant devoted to his community, who sold quality goods at a fair price, guaranteed all his merchandise, and constantly chased off hardware suppliers hawking inferior goods.

"All of this hard work and unselfish honesty meant that I never got rich. So, if I had one wish, I'd wish to be wealthy."

St. Peter, impressed by Dave's saga of sacrifice and humility, snapped his fingers, a wheelbarrow full of gold materialized, and off the shop-owner went into the streets of Heaven. No sooner had Dave gone than another man, Larry, appeared at the Gate. St. Peter explained the protocol, and Larry told his story. Coincidentally, he, too, had run a hardware store. However, the Larry took long vacations, bought shoddy tools and supplies from unscrupulous hardware salesmen, had to refund a lot of money for second-rate goods, and rarely could balance his books.

"So, anyway, I never made much money at it, so I guess I'd like to be rich," Larry said.

St. Peter was disappointed, even a little dejected, but this man hadn't been evil. St. Peter snapped his fingers, another wheelbarrow full of bullion appeared, and Larry strolled off with his gold. As he did, a third man appeared at Paradise's Pearly Portal. He began his spiel as soon as St. Peter paused for breath.

"I'm Joe, a hardware supply salesman for forty years. Made millions at it."

St. Peter looked slightly bewildered. "A hardware supply salesman? Do you also want a wheelbarrow full gold?"

"Heck, no," Joe said. "Just give me a wheelbarrow full of junk and show me where those two shopkeepers went."

We can laugh at the story, but, by the end of the day, Dave probably still had his gold, while Larry ended up with a wheelbarrow full of junk. Why? Because Dave held on to his power to choose, while Larry surrendered his power to the salesman.

For the majority of the population, financial peril comes to those, like Larry, who surrender their power. But exercising power requires work, and Larry didn't like work. To expect benefit without work is a child-like view of life. Children are provided for, or at least should be, but real adults, like Dave, provide for themselves. They do this by using their personal power; this is called responsibility. To expect entitlement, to think that security comes from outside yourself, from some benevolent act or agency, means you have abandoned your power to choose, to decide, to think for yourself. (This viewpoint is shown by our respect and honor for those who, keeping dignity and self-belief, succeed against the odds, compared to how we despise those who acquire wealth by other means, but are empty of virtue.)

Critical Combat

In the management world, power abhors a vacuum. That is, if a position of power has been abandoned, someone or something will step in and take that power. It's similar in personal finance: if you abandon your personal power, there are a million merchandisers ready to step in and divert your funds into their cash registers. And the invasion force they use is every sort of media channel available: consumer and fashion magazines, billboards, newspapers, TV ads, celebrity endorsements, distinctive branding, films, TV news, junk direct mail, spam, telemarketing, and the Internet. These are just a few of the dozens of ways producers of goods and services push their "buy" message deeply into all of our lives. Billions of dollars worldwide are spent in advertising, marketing, and merchandising; the moment a person neglects his or her decision-making power, these attack agents attempt to leap into the space and control that person's power to choose. (If you doubt this is true, pick up *The Hidden Persuaders,* by Vance Packard.)

So, then, how does one obtain, sustain, or regain one's personal power? One essential rule is *always ask "Why?"* Why do I want that? Why is it important to me? Why is that the price? Why will my day--or my life--be better for having bought it? Keeping one's mind on the true *reason* for things is more likely to keep fresh and accurate information in front of you than by asking "What do I want next?" or "Who should I hang out with?" And good information is fundamental to keeping your power. To ignore it is to surrender power. By contrast, accepting only the information that the commercial world presents to you is more likely to make you blind to the truth and blind to the fact that you're on a path to poverty. Keeping well-informed requires a bit of thinking, reading, and even debating. These things help keep the commercial world from convincing you to be somewhere, *or someone,* else.

Stunning hairdos, great suits, new skis, jewelry, teeth bleaching--all these things are fine in the right context, but don't become obsessed with images or choices that chase unreality, empty values, and false security. This is surrendering power.

Living With Your Decisions

Here's another story, a true one, about surrendering power. Many years ago when Lance Mason was living in New Zealand he was doing a series of 100-mile cycling rides to raise money for various charities. They weren't races, just group rides that fed off the enthusiasm of your fellow riders, sometimes up to 4000 of them. For one ride outside New Plymouth, on the North Island's West Coast, Lance stayed over the night before the ride with two Canadian friends, Doug and Lori. To cut an embarrassing story short, Lance bailed out of the ride halfway through, cycling back to Doug and Lori's, tail between his legs.

"Unlike the other rides I'd been on, it was windy, rainy, with only a small group of riders who quickly strung out along the course. No groups of eight or ten riders to pace-line or have a chat with, to try to enjoy what was otherwise a miserable day. In short, it was no fun so I quit.

"Back at the house, Doug was shocked. We'd both played rugby most of our (younger) lives. He was a committed athlete. Not a quitter. I didn't think I was, either. When I told him I gave it up because it was cold and boring, he clamped his hands over the ears of his two sons so they wouldn't hear these words of a spineless poltroon desecrating the sanctity of this home. I've never forgotten the embarrassment I felt.

"Gary Byrne did the Race Across America in 2006—a coast-to-coast 3000-mile team cycling race—and inspired a group from our club to do it in '07. I was the project manager and a member of the race team. It took eight months of intense bike training and organizational preparation. Fifteen racers and crew, our club, and a local charity we raised money for were relying on me to do it, and do it right. We trained in the cold, the wind, the rain, and the dark, on the flats, in the hills. We set our goals, made a plan, kept our eyes on the prize, did the preparation, and broke an age-group record for the race.

"The difference in the two episodes was my attitude and preparation. In the ride from Doug and Lori's house, I wasn't committed. I didn't prepare, except for some casual rides. There was nothing critical in it. To give it up, to let the weather and the boredom decide for me—that was easy, didn't take any effort. But my lack of willpower embarrassed me. It even embarrassed my friend Doug, and taught me a lesson about quitting. It's not just pride, ego, or the judgment of others. I had set out to do something and bailed out halfway through. I let myself down in my own estimation. I was a quitter—or at least could be."

The two stories are different. One ride was 100 miles—part of a day. The other was 3000 miles, more than a week, and months of preparation. One ride was alone, the other with a team. But they were both raising money for charity. In both, there was a goal, a decision, a choice that had to be made. "There was a time in both rides when I had to sling my leg over the bike and do the business—or quit. There was a time when I had to put my own personal power to work, or let forces outside myself take control and push me to the side of the road.

"I won't forget the ride I quit; I still feel an emptiness about that day. And I won't forget the one in which our team crossed the finish line after 3000 miles, setting a new record in the process. That day, that week, brings me ongoing rewards for what we, as a team, accomplished and for how my contribution helped in that victory."

The Strength of Your Adversary

In the section above, we made a lot of remarks about advertisers, marketers, and merchandisers, and how they'll take your power if you let them. But how do they really do it? Isn't what they do just the flip side of the "no entitlements" argument? In the same way that we have to set our goals and use our power to get what's good for us, aren't they allowed to set business goals and exercise their power to achieve what's good for them? Yes and no. Mostly no. And the reason is that so much of what they say is either *unproven, meaningless,* or simply *false*—deceptive claims that lead us to faulty decisions.   But because they have the commercial power--the money and the access to media--to distort marketplace information, they can control the knowledge the consumer receives and, so, have power over the consumer's decision-making process.   And that's what they do.   They fill the print media, the airwaves, the small screen, the big screen, and cyberspace with scientifically designed phrases, mottos, mascots, still images, film images, legends, myths, celebrities, and near-celebrities to brainwash the spending public into believing these products are essential to health, success, wonderful relationships, daily sex, life, liberty, and the pursuit of happiness. And fluffy laundry.

The Monster That Is Marketing

The operative phrase in the paragraph above is "*scientifically   designed,*"   because   marketing incorporates a tremendous amount of science.   The problem is this: it's not "consumer science."   The corporations are mostly *NOT* using the science of soap chemistry or automotive engineering to show how one product actually does its job better than its competitors at a fair price.   No.   The science they're using is the science of human behavior – the Dark Side of neuroeconomics – because it's your decision-making they want to control (to get you to buy what you often *don't need* at prices with *no relation to life's values)*.

And the behavioral sciences are very real, very powerful, and very dangerous. They're dangerous because, if merchandisers use them effectively, they can control how people think. If they can control how people think, they can dictate their choices. They can take away your power to control your life.

Whoa! Thought control? Brainwashing? This is all sounding too "science-fiction." Too *Matrix Reloaded.* How can a shampoo company make you believe that using their products will make you the belle of the ball? How can a car company persuade you that driving their pick-up truck will turn you into an action hero? The answer is <u>marketing,</u> the same hype-filled baloney that Big Tobacco used to convince generations of people that smoking wasn't bad for you.

What is *marketing,* and how is it different from *advertising?* Advertising just puts a product into media channels (TV, magazines, billboards, and so on.) with a message that says, subtly or otherwise, that this product will bring happiness or fulfill a need. Marketing is much bigger. It's the packaging, the feel, and the smell of the product, its claims of ease-of-use or success over the competition, quick access on the store shelves, association with celebrities or celebrity-like lifestyles, placement in feature films and public events for an "everyone loves this product" impact. It's the brand saturation, air-time attention, and in-the-flesh salesmanship. In the sales world, marketing is *everything you do.*

Marketing is manipulation of the consumer in the purchasing process, a manipulation spearheaded by intense use of every media vehicle: TV, cinema, print, signs from shop shelves to billboards, gift-with-purchase, junk mail, spam, Google, Amazon, Yahoo!, famous brands, publicity stunts, and on, and on. The methodologies run from highly specific targeting down to simple trial-and-error. They invade your day, your mind, and your thought processes, similar to the way a virus invades an organism.

A virus forces its DNA, its genetic instructions, into its victim's cells. From that point, the future of the victim is determined not by its own best interests, but by the virus's DNA which is now in command of the host cells. Much of what the organism will be and do is now set by what the virus put into those cells; the organism is no longer in control of itself. And the virus may work very hard at keeping itself hidden.

In much the same manner, the marketing industry spends millions of man-hours and billions of its clients' dollars to steal your power, to rob you of the freedom to do things in your own best interests, by trying to inject spending instructions into your life all day, every day, making you a slave of the three "m"s, media, marketing, and merchandising.. But, in a virus-like effort to remain undetected, the marketing industry spends a lot of clients' money to keep itself <u>invisible,</u> to hide from us the fact that we are being manipulated. It is crucially important that you don't know that your power of free choice is being hijacked. So don't be surprised if much of what we present seems farfetched at first.

But why does it work? Why do all these "tricks of the trade" actually get people to reach in their pockets and spend money? How does this multi-billion-dollar business of marketing actually take control of our free will and, in doing so, create a marketplace of force-fed consumption? How do they accomplish this fundamental theft of the buyer's ability to say no? "Brainwashing" is a better answer than you might think, because a big part of the explanation has to do with biology and chemistry of the brain.

Better Living through Chemistry

That most wonderful organ, the brain, produces chemicals called <u>endorphins</u> that most of us have heard about. To oversimplify, they can reduce pain (physical or emotional) or provide pleasure (physical or emotional), and can be triggered by things as diverse as eating jalapeño peppers to debating political opinions. This pain-no/pleasure-yes control is involuntary and can be addictive, literally biologically *addictive*. Science doesn't know why we have brains that do this, but it may relate to evolution and clan formation, where our prehistoric ancestors grouped together with like-minded others for mutual enjoyment and protection. Because of the fundamental role endorphin science plays in understanding human behavior, we will visit this topic frequently throughout the book.

We do lots of things that produce endorphins. Since they bring pleasure or reduce pain, it only makes sense that we would continue to do those things that produce them. A remarkable fact is that we produce endorphins when we talk to a person who agrees with us on something meaningful.   If a companion in a cocktail conversation sees eye-to-eye with us on White House policy, we enjoy that discussion. We enjoy it because it produces endorphins, creating a biologically pleasant effect that induces us to repeat or continue the activity. This is called *reinforcement,* and it applies to our attachment to motorcycles, hunting rifles, lip gloss, exotic teas, running shoes, or tanning salons. (The tobacco industry enjoys a double "addiction advantage," endorphins through marketing plus nicotine in the products.)

So what else reduces pain or produces pleasure by producing endorphins? *Shopping.* If we're emotionally down and we buy something that we perceive as desirable or rewarding, that can cause endorphin release, creating pleasure. Guess what? The marketing industry knows this.   How do they use this *information* (a primary source of power) to control our choices and, thereby, our lives? By combining billions of dollars with decades of experience in human psychology to fabricate an artificial world of beauty and contentment, put us in it, and then convince us that buying all the various products and services of this phony universe will make us as tickled pink as Bill and Peggy on TV who just bought a new car, ate a delicious and fun meal at a Greez-n-Pickle outlet, and got the grass stains out of little Jimmy's school trousers. All of this is aimed at structuring our outlooks so that buying the product *agrees* with our view of life, *stimulates* endorphin production, and makes us *enjoy* the purchase.

You've heard of "focus groups"? It's when a marketing company recruits a group of everyday schmoes like you and me to test out our endorphin rush from their clients' new SupaBurger or pomegranate juice or DVD player. All the focus group test-taking and questionnaires, and the marketing company's analytical posturing, are mostly geared to raise the advertising and marketing budget to the company's client. The real "nut" of the exercise is, "Did the customer enjoy the burger? Would the customer buy it and encourage her friends and family to buy it?" That's all the client cares about. Debates on trans-fats, Blu-Ray, sonic sound, dirt-eating enzymes – to the marketers, they're all promotional slogans and "spin." To the marketers, they're just words on a box, advertised justification for making the sale. What really matters is whether or not the customer *enjoyed* the product or service. Enjoyment causes reinforcement, repeat business, referral of others, and the ability to charge what the market will bear. Enjoyment comes from endorphin production and the pleasure they bring. The world of "sales enhancement" knows this; they work tirelessly to pull us into a world where they can communicate with our endorphin centers without interference or resistance from the thinking part of our brains.

Turning the Tide

The authors make no bones about the fact that our aim is to change your view of the world and yourself, to have you see the much greater benefits of keeping control of your life – and your money. Restructuring your perception of value and security will *reprogram your brain's endorphin production* so you will get less enjoyment out of wasting your money and more enjoyment out of reaching your financial goals.

Behavioral science and a long history of trial-and-error have given the merchandizing and marketing industries a huge beachhead in our brains. Our daily universe is saturated with the "buy" message, from the cereal box and the mouthwash bottle in the morning to ads on midnight TV, and everything in between.

Don't surrender your power to the corporate consumption world. To give up your power is to quit on yourself, and it comes from a lack of self-belief. Worse than losing some big battles can be surrendering small, daily ones. This is because there are so many more of them – they comprise the emotional and psychological momentum of everyday life. Later we'll discuss how things like invasive gambling, cheating, taking shortcuts, and get-rich-quick schemes are all examples of loss of self-belief. But for now, *Know Yourself, Grab Your Power,* and *Don't Let Go!*

PATH TWO

The Slow Leak

Poverty Road is paved with small expenses. Not that big expenses can't create a financial black hole. They can. But the way that *most* people find themselves in the red is through small, unnecessary spending, especially by habit, and particularly when purchase decisions are made in the past and not reviewed, ignored in some way. Here is the pattern: Find ways to spend small amounts of money three or four times a week, even every day, for things you don't need, things that add no lasting value to your life. Make the amounts small enough that

(1) you don't think about them much, but
(2) when you do, they're "too little to worry about," so
(3) you don't have much inclination to stop, and
(4) you feel okay about spending bigger amounts several times a month . . . or more.

Between paychecks, rarely watch what you spend, and then only so you don't have to run off to Bolivia to escape the debt collectors. If you time your purchases cleverly, you can spin this out for years, and then go flat broke with electrifying quickness, not having to suffer the long, drawn-out pain of cutting back on your lifestyle. Yes, of course, this sounds like someone you know. But not you. Right?

So, for those of you who have been snoozing through the early parts of this book (that talked about getting rich), waiting for the part that's going to tell you how to find your way to *true poverty,* this is it. It all starts here.

The Slow Leak

The truth is we, the authors, have been waiting for this part of the book, too, because we get to talk about bicycles. Riding bicycles is something near and dear to our hearts. It's how we met, and how our friendship has built over the years. Many of our best conversations have been on bikes, riding with our bike club, and sitting around afterward telling lies, half-truths, and authentic tales of the West over a bottle (or two) of wine. (A message for the Great Unwashed: the cycling club's house wine, from a local deli chain, and universally shunned by the spouses, is Charles Shaw, $1.99 a bottle – a.k.a. Two Buck Chuck. It was after one of these mid-week rides and a bottle of 2BC that we agreed to write this book.)

We're not cycling experts, but it's something we have a passion for, so it fits as a vehicle for a message in this book. Bikes are delicate performance instruments.

Strong and resilient, they are also dramatically sensitive to a couple pounds in weight, the pitch of a hill, or the air pressure in the tires. Vary these much, and the bike's performance will radically change.

Take air pressure. Ever ride a bike with a slow leak in the tire? Ride a mile, pump it up. Ride a mile, pump again. You might get where you're going, but it's a lot more work and a lot slower. One thing we've learned: stop and fix the leak at the beginning, and you'll reach your destination much faster, with less work, than if you let that leaky tire slow you down time and again on the way to your destination.

So, if we *were* in pursuit of poverty, as the title suggests, how can we be perfectly sure we'll be stone-broke some day? By using the method described at the beginning of this chapter – the money-mismanagement equivalent of the Slow Leak. By letting a few dollars slip through your fingers day after day, without looking twice at what's happening, you, too, could be on *The Second Path* to poverty.

The Road Out

However, if, by chance, you don't want to be poor, what should you do? To have money to invest, should you shun every pleasure that shopping has to offer and become a cave-dwelling hermit? No, of course not. But some "leaks" may need to be fixed, some expenses curtailed.

As an illustration, we could go back to the preface and use smoking again. But the preface has played its part, and smoking has been thrashed so often over the last couple of decades that it may be played out as an example. Anyway, the journey's lesson might be better found down other avenues.

How about junk food? Cosmetics? Music CDs? Computer games? Computer doo-dads? Motorcycle logo doo-dads? Motorcycle magazines? Fashion magazines? Fashion accessories? Boutique coffees? Coffee accessories? Fashionable boutique coffee accessories? The latest mail-order-catalogue costume-jewelry organizer? Organic kitty litter from the bark of 200-year-old rubber trees growing in the Costa Rican rainforest? New and improved scum-removing laundry gel with *Zix-Quix,* the Enzyme from Outer Space?

The truth is, ladies and gentlemen, there is virtually no end to what you can spend your hard-earned bucks on, thanks to Madison Avenue and a trainload of very scientific research into socio-emotional addiction and mass consumer feeding frenzies. So it's time to put the brakes on the merchandisers, marketers, and advertisers.

We gave you an example in Guidepost #1 about saving $100 and investing it at 10% C.R. for forty years. It grows to $4500. But if you change that $100 to $1000, it grows to $45,000. (See P. 16, Table II; $1000 at 10% for forty years = $45,259.) Now, $45,000's okay. *But* if you invest $1000 again in the second year, and the third, and keep on doing that every year, never taking any out, it will be worth $500,000 when you're sixty. That is, for $40,000 in savings – $1000 a year for forty years – you get $500,000 back at the end. That's the simple arithmetic, using the "secret of C.I." It took forty years, but you got a *1250%* total return. In the meantime, you had a full life.

Maybe you can put in only $500 a year. You'll still have $250,000 when you're sixty. With $2000 each year, you'll end up with $1,000,000. And $3000 each year would get you $1.5 million. (See P 54, Tables IV-VI.)

The Rule of 72

A little piece of math magic is the Rule of 72. Divide any compound interest rate into 72 and the result is the years it takes for money to double at that interest rate; e.g., earning 10% compounded, an investment will double in 7.2 years. At 6%, it will take 12 years to double. It works the other way, too: for an investment to double in 8 years, it must earn 9% compounded.

Hidden Treasure

So, your *goal,* your annual *target* on your financial bicycle ride to prosperity, is an amount of money that you can save and put into an investment this year and every year. Let's start with a goal of $1000.

Where are you supposed to get this $1000?

You already have it. Yes, you already have it, but it's doing a *slow leak* out of your hands and into the hands of McDonalds or Proctor & Gamble or L'Oreal or the Harley-Davidson accessories franchise—or maybe Big Tobacco. You earn it, pay taxes on it, but then you spend it on stuff you don't need. You're letting it leak

TABLE IV

Number of Years	Beginning Total	Annual Addition	Year End Total
1	0	1,000	1,000
5	4,673	1,000	6,163
10	13,852	1,000	16,302
20	53,799	1,000	60,433
40	454,676	1,000	503,286

TABLE V

Number of Years	Beginning Total	Annual Addition	Year End Total
1	0	2,000	2,000
5	9,346	2,000	15,615
10	27,702	2,000	32,603
20	107,596	2,000	120,862
40	909,333	2,000	1,006,552

TABLE VI

Number of Years	Beginning Total	Annual Addition	Year End Total
1	0	3,000	3,000
5	14,020	3,000	18,488
10	41,555	3,000	48,906
20	161,397	3,000	181,298
40	1,364,028	3,000	1,509,859

out of your "money tires." And not only are you
spending for stuff you don't need, it's stuff you don't
want. Oh, you think you want it. You even think you
need it. The Multi-Media Mass-Marketing Machine has
wormed itself so far into our minds and our value
systems that we genuinely believe that we can find
happiness by buying a pair of gym shoes. Not only that
the gym shoes can make us happy, but that we can't be
happy *without* the shoes, that the shoes are a necessary
part of being a whole human being. We *need* those
shoes. Our co-workers *need* those shoes. Our neighbor
across the street *needs* those shoes.

> *Oh! These wonderful shoes!*
> *These brand new wonderful shoes,*
> *Hooowwww'd I ever live without them?*
> *Caaaaan't you see how much I need them?*

Okay, it sounds like a stupid example, but not so many
years ago city kids were maiming each other in street
fights over a new pair of sneakers. You see what we
mean?

It's a fact: thousands of large-to-very large
companies here and around the world are hiring
hundreds upon hundreds of advertising companies,
spending billions and billions of dollars (that *we* paid
them) to sell us stuff *they* make and *we* don't need (you
want to talk about American jobs?). And that money
that leaks away from you, day in and day out, week in
and week out, year in and year out, is the money that
you should be investing so you don't end up under the
railroad bridge. This is one of mass-media marketing's
big secrets, how they work to keep us off our money-

bikes and on the *Consumer Express* – "Next stop! Poverty, U.S.A.!"

Need a big push? Uncle Sam will let you put $1000 (and more) away each year tax-free. So $20 a week, or $1000 a year, taken out of your wages and put into an IRA is what you invest with. $20 a week before taxes is only $15 or less of your after-tax income. So to save $20 a week, you only have to cut $15 off what you spend after taxes, *if* you direct the $20 pre-tax into an IRA. The SUPER-benefit of that method is that all the interest your money earns also doesn't get taxed until you start taking it out at retirement.

The (Slightly) Painful Reality

So, let's make a list of stuff we don't need but spend "small money" on, money that should be pushing you to your goal, the $1000 a year you're trying to save (yes, *save)* and invest at 10%. We don't want people to live lives of monotonous drudgery, "lives of quiet desperation" (Thoreau). But people should *think* about their "bike tires" and what they spend small amounts of money on. See, *paying attention* is what the marketing industry does NOT want you to do. They just want you to react, like a trained chimp or a circus dog. They don't want you to realize that a few dollars tossed out every day or so quickly adds up to $20 a week. *That's your goal* – $20 a week, $85 a month, $1000 a year (over forty years at 10% = $555,000 – not a fortune, but better than a poke in the eye with a sharp stick; and we know you can do better than that).

So, here we go:

1 less Customized Coffee per week	$3
1 less fast-food stop per week	$4
1 less energy drink, or 2 fewer sodas per week	$2
1 less beer at the pub per week	$4
1 less lotto ticket per week	$2
1 x bag lunch per week instead of buying it	<u>$5</u>
	$20

What? You thought this was going to be easy? You thought someone was going to just hand you half a million bucks when you're sixty?

So, let's try it a different way - *by the month.* Now, we don't like this because we want you on a short leash, doing this every week. It's too easy to kiss off the discipline and lose control unless you're trying to save a little something every week. But let's look at it anyway:

1 less music CD, *or* computer gadget, *or* lipstick per month	$15
1 less nail salon visit per month	$20
1 less dinner out (just your share at some local place)	$25
1 less bottle of wine	$15
1 less fashion or car magazine	$5
Wash your own car	<u>$10</u>
	$90

That's $1080 a year. As long as we're slicing and dicing, let's look at yet another version: rather than cutting, let's try "slimming" on our consumptions this *week:*

Carnations instead of roses	$5
Consolidate the car trips to save two gallons of gas	$6
Leftovers again, or other waste-cutting steps	$5
Shop for 2 or 3 bargains (food, toiletries, and so on)	$5
	$20

We can't tell you what to save money on. We don't know your life. You have a spouse or partner? You're a solo parent with kids? You're a heroin addict with a fixation on Porsches and private jets? Let's look at the first two; the third one's too hot to handle.

Spouse or partner: No marriage-and-family counseling here, we promise, but let's suggest that if you're working toward a financial goal, the person you're sharing your life with ought to be advised. They say the two things couples argue the most about are money and sex. Money secrets between partners create a recipe for a bitter and unsavory meal. Try to share your financial planning with your S.O. (As for the sex, we'll leave that for our next book.)

So, what? You don't think you can save $20 a week, even PRE-tax? (We think you *can,* but . . .). How about $16? $14? *Something!* If not $1000 a year, then $800. If not that, then $600. Set a goal. Save it and invest it in an IRA with before-taxes income. Get started. Don't put it off. Your future is today. A million dollars is waiting.

Re: kids, this isn't a book on parenting, but kids will get the savings idea if you explain it. They like to play. Make a game of it. Depending on the relationship, and their phase in life, they can actually get on board (as opposed to "bored") especially if there's something in it for them – hey, they're kids. Learning about money at an early age is a healthy thing. It can bring them power over an uncontrolled future of their own. Don't try to insulate them from every problem. Let them share your goals and efforts. (BTW - If they're too young to understand, they're too young to spend your money. And if they're between fourteen and seventeen, beat them until they submit.)

But this ain't you, we hear. You're single and on the make. And who wants to date, like, an accountant anyway? You want to impress the other side of the equation with your financial freedom, your *joie de vivre*, your flights of fancy *now,* not when you're sixty. Where's the machismo in this cost-cutting gig? Where's the sexy charm?

The truth is that if this thing is important to you, it will mean something to whomever you're trying to build a relationship with – assuming you are. And if you're not right now, there'll be a time when you will, and this program for financial security will be an important factor when you get there. Be prepared.

Still not interested? That's okay. A lot of people feel that way. That's why we chose the title we did. We'll dust off your spot under the railroad bridge.

Putting It Together

This message in this chapter is fundamental, universal, and simple: Small Money Makes Big Money over Time. Plug the slow leak – or leaks – now, and you will have a very big payday in the future. The ability to get relatively rich is widely, widely available in America. Enough money passes through the hands of nearly every one of us that, with a bit of sacrifice and game-strategy, and a tune-up in your perspective, you can live a life as full – some would say fuller – than you have right now, and have a secure and fun retirement (yes, we'll talk about earlier pay-offs, too).

We don't pretend that *everyone* who picks up this book can trim $1000 a year out of their current spending (though most have the ability to save more). The fact is that some people in this country who want to do well, and try, have it really tough, too tough for how it should be in a country as rich as ours. We may be able to help those people only a little bit. Some others don't do much at all for themselves, regardless of their means. We can't help them, and don't aim to try. But most people have the ability to adjust their lifestyles and cut $20 a week out of their herd of choices, head that $20 into the corral, and not really miss it at the chuck-wagon later. This doesn't have to be painful. The fact is you can turn this into a game, an exercise in self-esteem that you'll enjoy (think endorphins).

Where you go with this is up to you. Some of you have been looking for a push in this direction, and will now start saving and investing $800 to $1200 a year. Some of you have bigger dreams, and will find $40 to $50 a week, $2500 a year ($1.4 mil "in the bank" after forty years). Reader # 622, she's going to get with the program; she's going to find $40 a week, plus another

$100 a month on special savings, and she's going to kick in another $400 each on her birthday, Christmas, Easter, and Kwanzaa. That means her investment account is going to get a *$5000* kick from her every year, and when she's sixty she's going to be looking at $2.8 million in cash.

Some readers are going to get *so damn* charged up on investing that they're going to look for "new and interesting" ways to get "unheard of returns." That's right. The returns they're looking for are "unheard of" because they don't exist, at least not in the real world (ask a few Wall Street ex-cons). There is an unshakeable truth about investing: there is no free lunch when it comes to risk. All rewards carry an equivalent level of risk. If you are looking for BIG returns, be ready to accept BIG risks, and to live with the BIG negative outcomes when some go bad. And you don't *need* to chase moonbeams. You don't *need* to play craps with your hard-earned investment dollars. Look! You had to give up a year of O'Donnell's Laughing Lunches to get this $1000 in your account – Don't blow it on a "sure-thing" investment in a Liberian diamond mine. Check out #622: $5000 a year, 10% compounded, $2.8 mil at retirement. Get with the program, and be careful with your money (and watch for our next book).

BTW, politicians in Washington and your state will do their best for you, which is usually pathetic. Don't rely on Social Security. *You* look after yourself and your family. No one else will do it within a mile of how well you'll do it yourself. Plug the slow leaks, get some money together every week, and invest it.

"Policing" Inflation

Before going further, we want to say something about the boring subject of *inflation* (and you thought saving money was boring). Contrary to the view that inflation is an increase in the cost of goods and services, inflation is actually an increase in the supply of currency. When people have more to spend, they spend it. This increase in consumer demand puts pressure on the supply of goods and services, driving prices up. This leads to a rise in all sectors: production costs, incomes, interest rates, more prices – the whole lot, but not at the same time.

For instance, a big hurricane hits the Gulf, ruins the sugar crop, sugar prices rise, donut prices rise, the police demand higher salaries. The city borrows money (increases the currency in the system) to pay the police for the increased donut bill, so taxes go up, interest rates go up, mortgages go up, all salary demands go up. IT nerds, now earning more, join with police to buy more donuts, pushing up the price.

You get the idea. Inflation in donut prices is caused by increased police and nerd salaries (*too much money* in the system – stop laughing; it happens) chasing an insufficient number of donuts (too few goods – actually, it's goods *and* services, but we couldn't make the donut joke with services). So, yes, people, businesses, and so on are actually *competing* to buy things, and that drives up the price of everything. *But* the cost of all the stuff you used to buy but *aren't buying now* also goes up. So, yes, you actually save more money by not buying what went up in price. But you must then raise your weekly or monthly target amount, because inflation will mean you will need more retirement money. So you spend less, save more, and PRESTO! You have an inflation-proof retirement plan. See, we told you before, inflation doesn't matter. Much.

For those who find the donut story hard to swallow, here's another real-life example: the huge rise in housing prices around the Western world from 2002 to 2007. Why did it happen, and why did it all collapse? It happened because economies were strong, incomes were high, and money was easy to borrow – too easy. Banks promised people money in great bundles, with very few questions, and people used the money to go house-shopping. Even a building boom during this time didn't keep up with demand, so the flood of money drove up house prices, especially where supply was tight or demand high. When the flaws in these and other banking practices came to light, the credit mechanisms cracked under pressure, and lending and borrowing slowed to a trickle. The loss of easy money undercut the upward pressure on prices, and they fell – a lot.

So inflation wasn't just the rise in housing prices, but the rise in easily available money chasing the supply of houses – too much money in the system. What does this mean for you? The more money you borrow to buy the things you think you want, the more the cost of those things will rise. Use restraint. Discuss the purchase with a loyal friend who has different tastes. Does it fit with your values?

Green Money

We haven't mentioned much about "green" economics, but it's a tremendous force in the world now. Colleagues, co-workers, and commentators all told us we must be caught talking about it. Obviously, anything to do with conservation of resources, cutting down waste, and controlling future costs relates to saving money, so to whatever degree a green viewpoint or interpretation contributes to your savings in the near, medium, or long term, we're in favor of it. The wider social and political opinions and stances that debate the protection of nature, economics, and mankind's legacies are a challenging topic on their own and we're not going to tackle them in this book.

Still, there are practical examples to consider. Don't waste water, food, or clothing. Don't waste electricity and gas. Think about your driving trips. Can something be fixed rather than replaced? Is packaging required; can we discourage it? How paperless can we be? In our town, we're not charged for collection of recycling waste, but we are for landfill waste, so we try to reduce the latter in favor of the former. Hanging the washing instead of using a dryer saves gas or electricity (but one community in our town prohibits residents from hanging out the washing!).

So, "green" consciousness can be a money-saver, too, so we didn't want to neglect it as another possible route to building up your bank account.

The new "green" world, however, has one significant philosophy that marries well to an old philosophy in the world of consumer goods: when you can, buy quality. Well-designed and well-made goods that last longer and perform better are often greener *and* more economical than shoddy goods.

A simple example of this arose recently with a friend we'll call Jack. Jack bought a manual orange juicer on the internet. It was marketed by a kitchen-goods retailer and was similar to what his parents had had in the 1950s – or so it looked. It seemed priced fairly at $40, and arrived quickly. After two weeks of use, the mechanism proved faulty and the materials second-rate. Jack had to struggle to make it perform its basic function: to juice oranges.

Jack complained to the retailer, got his complaint kicked upstairs to the supplier, and, lo and behold, they sent him a replacement. Guess what? Same story: lousy juicer.

But our boy Jack is tenacious. He emailed the supplier's customer service, the supplier's founder, and the supplier's head of marketing. (Since the machine is manufactured half a world away, the supplier is simply an importer – a middleman.) Jack got a reply from the supplier's CFO making claims for his company's integrity, product quality, etc. The CFO's main defense: "Our juicers really are good, and you can't get anything good made in America any more." Ergo, it's okay to move resources to China, make the juicers there, import thousands (millions?) of these junky things back from China, sell them on the Web to Jack and his mates, and populate landfills with them. To insure Jack was a "satisfied customer," the CFO offered to take the two low-level juicers back and send Jack their next level "super" juicer. Jack figured they must have a lot of these things lying around.

This ain't green, ladies and gentlemen. When you buy, try to buy good quality stuff.

*   *   *

Probing further into The Slow Leak

So let's say your long-term goal is to retire at sixty with an extra $500,000 cash (on top of any other retirement assets). You must calculate how much you have to save and invest, beginning now. If you're twenty-one, you need to save and invest $1000 every year until you're sixty. But if you're forty, you have nineteen fewer years to grow the pot, so you must salt away much more each year (examine our various tables and use the twenty-year growth span figures). You can also consider working until sixty-five, which gives you five more years to save. . . .but, alas, five fewer years to live after retirement (sorry!). Our preceding tables show the outcomes for various contributions over varying years of saving and investing.

But the basic facts remain the same. You need to invest something every year, and, unless you already have surplus income, you need to rescue that "something" from your spending. So, *yes, it's true,* buying things you don't really need is a leak in the tire of your financial bicycle.

For instance, Jack has a free half hour twice a month, a sponge, and a bucket, but pays someone else

$20 a month to wash his car. Slow leak – $20 less for his savings. Getting to his investment goal is going to take a little longer and be more work.

Reader: "Oh, spare me – $20? Who can't afford $20 a month on innocent purchases and still save enough toward their goal?"

Well, we're glad you're in that income bracket, Sunny Jim. Some people aren't. But it's only $20, not a lot, we agree. Let's put another little hole in the tire: $20 a month on Customized Coffee "extras." So, that's $20 + $20. Twice the leak, twice the pumping, twice the obstacle to your goal. Still, that's only a savings of $40. So let's try to find a C-note every month, say $600 spent over six months on stuff you didn't need:

1. January - $180 for the new season's J.J. Beansworth miracle-fabric rain-proof James Dean-replica windbreaker, in Spring Cherry
2. February - $60 on the "revolutionary" skin-toner
3. March - the latest video game + the new "Raving Monkey" CD: $40 + $15
4. April - $100 to $200 on the new shirt- or blouse-and-trousers combo
5. May - $80 at the nail salon + $20 super-sized fast-food (c'mon, just for *May*)
6. June - $20 to $100 on the new computer gizmo

That's $515 to $695. Call it $600 total for six months, $1200 for the year. Over your goal by $200. And we've just snatched a few things out of the air. It's not our job to itemize your life. That's *your* job. There's nothing in this list you can't live without. You name your own poison – how, where, and how much – goods or food or services you sort of felt you really needed but knew you really didn't. Because if you have enough leaks, it's big trouble. The tire leaks faster than you can pump it up. No goal, no savings, no investment. And the U.S. Government isn't going to come looking for you to give you a condo on Santa Monica Beach.

Eve, Adam, and the Serpent of Hope

Of course, the one small gorilla in the (bedroom) closet that no one – meaning us – has mentioned yet is the male-female shopping dichotomy. As males, the authors admit feeling alien to the female shopping experience. And we understand that it is an *experience,* a cultural ritual through which women immerse themselves in behavior that, in the best interest of our book sales, we won't try to explain. (Please direct all hate-mail to our editor.)

But let us balance the scales. In truth, *feeling* alien to the ritual and *being* alien to it are entirely different things. Because, in our view, men shopping and women shopping are peas in a pod. For every Angie and Lois gossiping about Valerie's extramarital affairs while dumping a grand on Manolo Blahniks, Rudy and Jeff are bragging about discount surf trips to La Paz, while one of them shoots $5K on an Italian racing bike. Come on, if he wanted exercise, he'd ride the old balloon-tire cruiser – *that's* a workout!

Truth is – men *and* women – they're buying the same thing. *Hope.* Hope, image, and status with their peers. And there's nothing wrong with that *IF* they're taking care of business on the savings side. Set your goals, stash the dough, reach your target, then you can spend all you like (*within* your *means*). And, in fact, that is a very intelligent way to go about this game of building your "fiscal retaining wall" for your later years, and we'll work our way back to that. (For anyone who thinks men don't "shop," hang around a surf shop, a fishing tackle shop, or a motorcycle dealer.)

Biking in the Mirror

It goes without saying – we hope – that saving money for the future is incompatible with running your credit cards to the limit or writing bad checks. Unless you want to spend your retirement money from inside Folsom Prison.

Which brings us to a discussion of *priorities*. You're on your bike riding across town to collect your $500,000, but you need to keep the bike moving at this speed or faster, and stay on it until you get there. If you can do that, you can retire early, and you'll be set up for life. The problem is all these donut shops along the way. And coffee shops. And clothing stores. And fishing tackle outfitters. And in front of each one is a pile of broken glass. So when you stop to shop, you get another little leak in one of your tires. That slows your bike down, so you have to pedal harder because of the new leak, and pedal faster because of the time you lost shopping . . .*IF* you're going to get across town in time to collect all the moolah.

So, the "priorities" bit is the boring old question of what's more important, A or B or C or D. Do you want to hoist your Manolo-shod feet in the mall for the afternoon, have a cup of Buddha-tree coffee, do iPod to Raving Monkey, and have your nails done, or can you live with half that, and bike a little closer to your goal? Study and give importance to the genuine priorities in your life. If you're going to set goals and be ready to pay a price for reaching them, you have to be ready to *take* the important choices and *pass* on the not-so-important choices. If you can do that, you're coming to understand yourself, the most important thing in your life to know. This is the lesson of the Japanese mirror.

Variations on the Theme

Now, at the risk of making an absolute laughing-stock of this "financial bicycle" analogy, we're going to push it one notch farther, in hopes of pulling in a few more readers. Over there, across town, up the hill, or over the bridge, is the $500,000 waiting for you. Okay, so what happens if you're late? And what does "being late" mean? Well, being late can mean several things, and it may not be so bad (though not getting there at all is a total loser).

If "late" means you pedaled slow because you had a lot of leaks or were just lazy (didn't put much money away each year or had no willpower), then you'll have to pedal longer and harder (work and save for more years) to get to the $500,000. Or if "late" means you started later than someone who started saving and investing sooner, then again you'll have to pedal-work longer in life, or pedal-save more each year, or both. Or if you started biking early, and saved and invested well, but then bailed from the program and blew all the money on night-life in the fast lane, then you may have to start over with a broken bike (and a scarred and battered body), a steep uphill in front of you, and not a lot of years to get it all back. The choice is yours. You already got our advice.

So, let's revisit socking the money away early, what we like to call the "no more homework" idea. This is when you do the hard yards at the beginning, and then can relax and enjoy the rest of the week. Pedal really hard and far, maybe uphill, and then coast for a while. Let's say you're doing the $20 a week thing. You scrimp and save and have $20 "in the cookie jar" by mid-week, then – no more homework! – you buy what you want the rest of the week. Or you can save $40 one week, then relax the next week (but never so much that you ding last week's savings, *or* next week's). Then do the same thing the next two weeks, if you want. Or you're on a $100 a month investment plan, so you "bank" $200 this month, and "party up" the next month, then go back to the regular plan. If you're shooting for $1000 each year, you could buckle down and save up a grand between January and June, then enjoy some leisure between July and December, keeping enough aside for your Christmas shopping.

Cautions: We're not too happy about the last idea. The second six months, July – December, without the discipline of saving-investing, can weaken anyone's resolve and break good habits. It's only for those who really have the willpower to set the saving game aside for a long period and go right back to it when it's time. Otherwise, we want you on a short leash – no more than a month without saving, and preferably no more than two weeks. And – this is *critical,* of course – you can *never, never, never* do this in reverse. You can never say, "Well, I'll spend up large this week and save twice as much next week." That's a *Seven Paths* absolute No-No. You don't know what's going to happen next week or next month. Put the cash in the bank while you have it.

Sister Carol Anne

As Lance Mason's fourth grade teacher, Sister Carol Anne, said, "Procrastination is the thief of time." Economizing to save capital is hard work; delaying that work steals the time you need for your savings to grow. This gets to the heart of how you view and pursue *gratification.* *Deferred* gratification means dodging some fun now so you can do the work that will bring a lot more fun later. *Immediate* gratification is when you just dodge the work; you *procrastinate.* Overcoming that temptation through a combination of goals, willpower, and keeping your eyes on the prize will maximize the benefits of compound interest if you start early, and make it a lot less work later to reach your goal. The longer you put off starting, the harder it will be later to ever catch up.

Where the Rubber Meets the Road

It's time to get another list together, to rattle the cages of a few readers we missed. Who out there has spent more money on an H-D TV this year than you have on your financial goals? Who has more than one (two at the most) pair of running shoes? Who has three or more pairs of eyeglasses, mostly for show? You pay for the gym (instead of running, walking, riding, or doing push-ups); do you use it?

Plan your car trips to save a little gas. Turn off the lights you don't need at home. Get the new super-didj bike computer next year. Buy a half dozen Cokes, Pepsis, or Sprites instead of a dozen. Wear a light sweater instead of turning up the heat. Shave a few restaurant meals; don't order what you can't reasonably eat. Do without the extra glass of wine, cappuccino, or special dessert. Stop throwing edible food away, at home or out. Eat leftovers more often. This could all be $120 to $150 a month now, or more.

So take $150 you didn't need to spend. That's $1800 a year. Invest it every year from thirty to seventy, at 10%, compounded: $1 million.

So, if this is such a great thing, why isn't everybody doing it? Because most of them are buying $20 car-washes, $150 sneakers, $20,000 Harley Davidsons, and Soccer Mom SUVs when they can't afford to pay off their Visa bill, which they run up to $3000 to $5000 per month buying what they don't need.

Look, we know this is not always easy. Your co-worker just bought, leased, or inherited a new car. Your car is old. Cars, like kids, wall-to-wall carpet, and trees, change when you're not looking.   Paint fades, upholstery stretches and wears, the once-rhythmic ride is now like roller-skating over a lava field, the "symphony exhaust" sounds like gangsta rap in a traffic tunnel. And here's Jack's or Jill's new BMW, Lexus, or whatever, with "Moon Over the Sierras" paint, Veuve Cliquot leather, engine noise of a famished tiger, and you're asking yourself, "Why not me?"

The answer might be "Because you can't afford it." (This is different from when your plumber tells you that you need to save your house and the procedure is going to cost $2000 and you say, "I can't afford that." Which might be true. Or it might mean, "I don't want to spend my new color TV money on the plumbing.") We're talking now about the case where you really can't afford a new car and stay safely within the bounds of your income, your genuine needs, and your savings goal. Believe it. There are some things that you can't afford. A new car (or laptop, or set of china, or drapes, or jacket, or jewelry, or (boo hoo) bicycle, or vacation, or plastic surgery) might be one of them.

For now. Because the point of this strategy is that by taking control of all your small expenditures when you're young, thinking about how you spend, and getting an investment program going early, by the time you're in the peak of your earning years, you will have built up such a solid financial base that giving yourself some material rewards will be far more realistic.

Let's back up and look at a car purchase seen through sensible finance.   You're thirty years old.

You're debating about changing cars, moving up. You could drive yours for another year or two or three, but you're really drooling over this badass ride at the car lot, the salesman is talking a hot deal, but you'd need to sell or trade-in your car and come up with $10,000 cash. Let's look at the possibilities.

Scenario 1. Say you're up-to-date with your savings goal for the year, your job's solid, and you've got the cash in the bank. Looks like a no-brainer – you buy the car.

Scenario 2. You don't have the cash, you're barely reaching your savings goal, but your job is good and you can qualify for a low-interest $10,000 car loan. Buy? No. Your goal priority is a secure retirement, not a flash ride. Wait another year or two until you've got more cash.

Scenario 3. You don't have the cash and, though your job's OK, you're behind in your savings. No questions: keep your old car until you can afford your basic living costs *and* your savings, *and* you've got some extra cash, then go car shopping again.

(Just for thrills, let's rethink Scenario 1. You're age thirty with $10K in the bank. You invest $2K and spend $8K on a car. The $2K would be worth $34,000 when you're sixty. Or you keep $5K in the bank, invest $5K, and drive the old car until you can save another $5K; the $5K you invest at age thirty would grow to $88,000 by age sixty. Or you put off changing cars for two or three more years and invest the whole $10,000; at age forty, it would be worth $26,000 and you could really splash out for a fancier car. If you invested the $10K until you're sixty, you'd have $176,000, enough for a new Ferrari. Just so you know.

Keep in mind: if you spend the whole $10K now, especially if you stretch to do so, in three or four years you may be back car shopping and have to extend yourself again. Isn't it better to "get by" now and build up some cushion so you can really afford something great later?)

Eyes on the Prize

The basic lesson here and through this whole book is: savings are part of your basic costs, not a luxury, and you don't indulge your fancies until you've met the basics. But the truth is that if public transport isn't happening in your town, and going from A to B is part of your life, you need a car. If so, even your savings might have to wait. But be frugal. Keep your eyes on the prize. Plan for the savings, even if you can't make them yet. We know some of you are going to have to make some sacrifices and life changes to make this whole thing happen for you. It's not easy to get the thing in gear when you're starting from Square One. But you can do it. The benefits are out there to be seized.

PATH THREE

Push-Button Spending

This, the third path to poverty, is paved with microchips. Buying goods and services via electronic means, or "push-button spending," is replacing the use of cash and checks in the US and overseas. *Personal e-commerce* has become, at best, a popular time-and-money manager or, at worst, an easy route to a financial meltdown. Let's review the history.

Shopping Cops

Even before e-commerce, money didn't always change hands at the time of purchase. Fees for doctors, lawyers, and other professionals have always been billed; monthly payments were (and are) the general rule for mortgages, house insurance, school tuition, and car payments. You paid them on time or you were branded a bad risk, a bad debtor, services got cancelled, goods were repossessed, and/or you were pulled into court.

However, for most essential but "small money" purchases (consumable goods like food and gas, and clothes, transportation, utility bills, and the like), cash or check was the order of the day. If you qualified for credit or were known to the merchant, you might have had a "charge account" at the shop, paid monthly. If you didn't pay, your credit stopped. This marketplace usually distinguished essential (e.g., food) from nonessential (e.g., skydiving) expenses. Credit for the latter was harder to come by, and merchants generally looked askance at people who used it too freely. A shopkeeper or small business owner who heard "Send me a bill" too often could start restricting your purchases. In large segments of the commercial world today, *this balance* between credit risk and consumption, between merchant caution and buyer discretion, *is gone*. Why? One *HUGE* reason: credit cards.

Plastic Fantastic and the Credit Vampires

A signed credit card slip cancels the merchant's risk. He gets paid if he delivers the goods. So the more he can sell you, the more he collects, regardless of your *ability to pay* for that nuclear-powered espresso machine. Is there any incentive for the saleswoman not to sell you that Hermes scarf because your credit card is already $2000 or $10,000 in debt? None! "Oh, sorry, dear, your Visa seems to be at its limit. Have you got a MasterCard? Discover Card? American Express? Another Visa?" Then it's up to the card company to collect, and they are huge and powerful, with a library of information on you, from the size of your shirt collar to your preference in breakfast food. They will find you and get their pound of flesh, or ruin you in the process.

So, when using credit today, the buyers' game is much riskier. Instead of running up unpaid debts of $400 to $500 and making enemies of the local merchants, you make $5000 and $10,000 enemies of multinational vampires – credit card companies – who can suck every drop from your fiscal blood-bank and lock you into *years* of indebtedness, ruining your financial future. How are they able to do this? Because we surrender our power to them. We ask them to *act for us at the cash register,* to be our parent, until we can pay our own bills. We're adults. Is this rational?

And interest rates? *Usury!* People used to go to prison for charging what credit card companies do. So, if the merchant's risk is gone, and the card issuers are getting rich on the interest, who's going to stop you-the-consumer from buying more, multiplying your debt, and crippling your chance of future wealth? Only you. And the Corporate Universe have gone *totally* out of their way to see that you don't.

WARNING – Compound interest on *your debts* can work against you. Example: if you use a credit card and don't pay it off each month, the unpaid principle accumulates interest. If you don't pay everything off the next month, any unpaid interest adds on to any unpaid principle, and now they both accumulate interest. The interest on the debt is *compounding,* and the compounding is going *against* you. Making full credit card and other debt payments every month should be a high priority.

Smoke and Mirrors

As we talk, keep examining the *idea,* the *concept,* of the credit card, a real – and *virtual* – device for making a person's spending limits appear to disappear. The card is "real" because you carry it around and pull it out when you buy stuff. It's "virtual" because, at the check-out counter, it only *appears* that you're spending your own money. You don't. The merchant pushes some buttons and you spend the card company's or the bank's money. Only later, when you pay the credit card bill – *if* you pay it – do you spend *your* money. And if you don't pay it in full, you are borrowing money at huge interest rates and jeopardizing your financial safety. How much you have in the bank or in your pocket no longer dictates how much you can spend. Again, is that rational? No. If you run out of cash, you're just broke; but if you run up more on your credit card than you can pay, you're super-broke. It's a total loss of control and responsibility. "Living beyond your means" is the infamous phrase.

Ring – Ring – Ring. "Hello. I'm Not Home – Please Leave a Message."

"Hello. This is The Credit Police, and the message is 'Your debts are more than your assets and we've just repossessed your car, your house, and your life.'"

As we were about to go to press we read an article about a woman who left New York, going west in a succession of moves, trying to get out of deep debt from a NYC credit-card lifestyle. She ended up in LA and wrote a book about her monetary misadventures. The article quoted one of her NYC colleagues, an editor for one of the top three weekly U.S. news magazines, commiserating with her friend: "Who can't relate to running up credit card bills?" We found this gut-churning, that a mature, successful executive for a national news publication finds it common behavior to live on credit card debt, as though it should be expected.

We like a story from William Paulin, Ph.D., owner of Paulin Neal Global Business Development. "When my wife Sandy and I were students, young and broke, we tried to always pay our cards off every month. If we ever missed, the card we didn't pay off went into a locked desk drawer until it got paid off. To this day, though our finances are bulletproof, we still pay all our cards off every month. Maybe that's *why* we're bulletproof."

The simple lesson here is the same one we've been selling from the beginning of the book: Keep thinking. Keep your financial eyes open. Don't let the commercial world play you for the fool and part you from your money – and your goals.

Pandora's (Cash)Box

When credit cards were invented in the 1950s, no one knew how they'd change the entire landscape of purchasing and personal debt. But once cards caught on, the Three Ms – Media, Marketing, and Merchandising – realized they'd hit the big time. If they could combine "virtual" spending, the Information Age, and the hypnotic pleasure of "shopping endorphins," who knew where the spending patterns of the modern world might go? Exactly! *Who knew?*

Of course, not all aspects of spending-on-credit are bad – far from it. Credit cards and automatic bank payments, rationally and cautiously used, can be a boon to budgeting, safety, and efficiency. But for every person who uses them this way, how many lose their boundaries and create financial hardship through excessive credit? The ever-expanding complexity of this process today is hard to grasp. "Ripple effect" is too mild a term. It's more like a massive spending disease. Though it has slowed since the onset of the 2008-09 recession, the underlying – and ongoing – causes of this "credit contagion" have not. Diverse and ingenious are the methods the marketplace uses to get at your money.

Smart cards –

Who can feel stupid using something called a "smart card?" But you pay for goods or services before you receive them. *Way* before, usually. Great for the merchants – they get your money up front. Maybe you take delivery, maybe you don't. Maybe now, maybe later. Maybe never. And by "recharging" smart cards from credit cards, you open the doors to spending a little wider.

Cell phones –

Nothing new about buying things over the phone, right? Now with video screens, touch-pads, and web service, the world of commerce comes to your mobile phone so you can spend while driving to the credit counselor.

Bank account auto-debits –

Set it and forget it. Sounds good. Tell your bank to automatically pay your mortgage, your utilities, your car payment. . . your gym membership . . . your cell phone . . . your gas card . . . your credit card bill. With a little advance planning, you might have something left for groceries.

Credit card auto-debits –

Speaking of your credit card bill, in addition to all your one-off "plastic" purchases, you put three or four automatic monthly payments on your card and never look back. These are "buys" that stay on until you actively remove them. Take your pick: wine club, movie club, book club, dating club, cigar club, gourmet pears, Omaha steaks, computer anti-virus definitions, other indispensable software upgrades, skin emollients, fishing tackle, music CDs, magazine subscriptions, costume jewelry, lingerie from a bazaar in Azerbaijan, commemorative china, memorial coins, tarot card readings, and correspondence courses in Thai kick-boxing.

We were told this by a well-off fifty-something CEO: "Micro-buying for apps, ringtones, music, and the like on simplified click systems is an insidious invasion of one's financial home. I set a horrible example. I have probably click-bought 50 items in the last month; a year ago I bought zero. We thought 'connected' meant we were hooked to the web. What it really means is we're hooked to the world's cash register. Electronic merchandizing is emerging as a massive commercial force, and it has complete access to us even when we're mobile. Excuse me while I drown my cell phone."

How to Control It

In jest, we call pre-programmed card or bank account payments *Grand Theft Auto-pay*. It's actually a great concept. Millions of smart people use it. It's green. It saves time, stamps, envelopes, lateness anxiety, and monotony. It can streamline bookkeeping. But, without sensible rules about what goes on (and what comes off) your card or your account, it can also multiply and magnify fiscal distress.

Rule #1: Set-it-and-forget-it is a good method for de-fragging your computer drives, but not for overseeing your expenses. Re-evaluate the "spends" every 2 or 3 months. Are you building up a year's supply of Nebraska beef in your deep-freeze? Would your new husband prefer you to drop the internet dating club? Have you joined AA, making the monthly Wine Club shipments an approach-avoidance dilemma?

The "Three Ms" love auto-pay. They want you to spend in a no-look, hands-off process, what we might call "default-purchase merchandising," where the buyer and the original purchase decision become disconnected from any cash reality. We stop thinking about it. We suspend the repetitive, hands-on doling out of funds, each episode preceded by the bothersome – but responsible – choice to buy or not. Soon, the expenditure is a fixture in one's life. That's what the corporate world wants: no review, no reflection. They want to sell you on the idea once – *just once* – and then have you forget about it, while your auto-payments continue to roll out of your account and into theirs.

Impulse buying

This is another marketing thrust where button-pushing is critical, only this time it's *your* buttons that are being pushed. While the technique of impulse buying is no secret, merchandizing still relies on it. You love chocolate? Guess what they have next to the register. But not everyone is susceptible to impulse buying, and the sales industry knows this, too. So they orchestrate the entire devilish symphony around a multitude of factors to maximize inventory turnover and store profits.

Every item in the store competes with every other item for your dollar, and the *shelf positions* that return the biggest profits get the most marketing attention. *Bar-coding* provides high-speed, high-accuracy *data* to the store management and the distributors. Data plus miles of *sales research* make *information* from which to structure the *presentation* of goods to achieve the highest product turn-over. The cashier area is the last line of attack before you make for the exit, so they ramp up the exposure as you reach for your wallet or purse. A little urgency, less time to think, and the same story comes into play again – endorphins. Can they find a celebrity mag, an anti-freeze brand, or a style of peanuts that tickles your fancy in that certain way so your brain says, "Ooo, yeah – I'll take some of that, too," on your way out the door. Not quite enough cash? Put it on the card. One more sale.

Locking-up The Sale

A perfect fit for impulse selling is the immediacy of web-buying. Point-and-click equals button-pushing – so simple, so quick and easy. No time needed to think or analyze. No deferral of gratification. Jump now!

However, for web-based shopping, the "impulse" plays just a supporting role. Using one-click credit-card sales, the commerce machine has *the* super-slick internet purchase method to go with media saturation and marketing science. Shopping from home, a place where your viewpoints are already reinforced, can be an endorphin-rich experience (though the important social component of shopping is lost). Moreover, TV, the computer's evil twin, is there to help sell, and no travel is required.

The computer is a great channel for marketing *provided* the marketers can win the IT information war and overwhelm the careful buyer. Traditional penetration tools – questionnaires, gift-with-purchase, bulk- or multiple-purchase discounts – are easily employed, while some irksome customer habits like canceling purchases after "closing" and returning merchandise are much reduced. Credit card details can be permanently logged into a site for ease of purchase and "same store" loyalty. Talk about synergy. Talk about self-directed spending. Talk about targeting an audience. Talk about unnecessary spending. The information cyber-power that industry has is nearly unending.

As we were going to press, Megan McArdle, *The Atlantic*'s financial editor, published a superb article on the ramped-up, highly refined world of the dominant TV shopping channel. From her personal visit to the channel's HQ and subsequent research, McArdle slices and dices the power, sales-science, and success of this 50-million-customer retail push-button monster, a true "marketer" that can get you to buy perfume on TV when you *haven't even smelled it first!* Now *that,* ladies and gents, is a "media sale" without parallel.

Another inventive way to snatch your scratch? Penny internet auctions, where the bids are 1c or 2c, but you have to pay to 30c-50c-70c for every bid you make. The total fees collected in any one successful sale may be many, many times that sale (or purchase) price of the item offered. But the system spreads those fees over hundreds or thousands of bidders so no one notices the fortune in bidding fees. *Time* gave an example of an item that sold for $100.01 in a 1c-per-bid auction, in which each bid cost the bidder as much as 60c to place. So over $6000 in bidding fees could have been collected for an item that retails for a few hundred.)

Checks and Imbalances

It could be said this all began thousands of years ago with money, little symbols you put in your pocket and took to the market to buy stuff with, instead of carrying your goat or wood carvings or aged grape juice around looking for someone to trade with for a new Corvette.　More likely, though, it began a couple centuries ago when a smart marketer thought, "Maybe we can reduce buying resistance by disconnecting the purchase from the conscious act of spending cash. Substitute pieces of paper for real currency and they won't worry so much about what they're spending." Thus was born the checking account (and the immortal line, "I can't be out of money – I still have checks in my checkbook").

CMP ("critical merchandising point"): If we can separate "buying" from "spending" in the consumer's mind, we accomplish two things: reduced awareness of overspending; purchase value becomes less important. Hence, we can sell you lots of unnecessary junk.

Every avenue of selective media marketing sells stuff we don't need and fights to instill in us an image that compels consumption to fulfill that image. This is a scientific application of Maslow's first hierarchy of need: self-actualization. If you can manipulate the self-image, you can aim your product or service at that image.

Thus we return to Maslow's Hierarchy of Needs and to endorphins. We cannot over-emphasize their role in personal life. All human motivations, choices, and actions (and regrets) stem directly or indirectly from them. Any debate on their specifics isn't the point. The truth is there: the most successful and enduring motivation is self-actualization, acting to fulfill the vision you have of yourself. The second motivation is peer-based acceptance and reward. They both cause a pleasure response in the brain. If a culture of inbred marketing can plant in a population with money a pattern of thinking based around a glistening self-image encrusted with the material adornments and luxuries of a consumption-based existence, then the marketing owns the people. They become the machine of consumption for the marketers' industrial clients.

Return to Earth

Aren't there any silver linings here? Yes. ATMs and bank account auto-payments have one big positive: you can't spend what you don't have. That doesn't prevent you from spending what you do have on stuff you don't need, but at least you can't go deeply in debt doing it that way. *Unless* your friendly bank has attached some sort of credit line to your account. Be careful.

Since endorphins bring pleasure, they can be used in your favor. You can become engrossed in your goals, in your constructive self-image, and in your motivation to be financially secure, and all the acts you perform to achieve that vision have endorphin potential, reinforcing the goals and your pursuit of them. For instance, you can set up an auto-payment from your regular bank account, or maybe from your credit card, into a savings-and-investment account; every time there's an investment deposit, you get a rush. When you go out to spend, leave "the card" home; go back to spending cash, the "real world" money. This will re-work your spending endorphins so cash gives the rush instead of a credit card.

Think. Don't let the marketing and merchandising world take your authority away. Relish your decision-making rights and power. Enjoy life, but within the boundaries of what's real, not what the media tries to tell you is real. If you do this, you future will be more secure. Endorphins will flow.

PATH FOUR

"But I Deserve It!" and Other Fallacies

As we reach the mid-point of the Seven Paths, we want to revisit the fundamental fact underpinning this book, the truth to which all of our approaches return: Nearly everyone in America has enough money pass through their hands from childhood onward to be financially secure by the age of sixty. It only needs conscious management and cutting down on mistakes. For most of us, this will require keeping our goals in focus, self-control in spending, and some confidence that we are doing the right thing for ourselves.

With these three strengths we can turn a small amount of weekly savings into a large, secure retirement fund. Without them we fall into the patterns that slowly but surely diminish our shot at security. This chapter's path to poverty parallels the simple human tendencies toward competition and self-gratification, and shows how the marketing industry's genius for image-saturation has bred an "I deserve what I want" mind-set that outstrips incomes, fosters status-seeking life-styles, and memorializes a sense of luxury entitlement raised in previous chapters.

Chasing the Never-Never

Everyone reading this page knows the meaning of "keeping up with the Joneses." It refers not only to conspicuous consumption, but *competitive* consumption. Some would argue that "the Joneses" phrase is too trite to warrant the space, to deserve its own section. But this is the very reason to focus on the "Jones" angle: it seems trite because competition has been part of human social behavior since before the Bible, and societies throughout history have tried to control or shape that competition. Why? Because, depending on what it's based, competition can be either productive or destructive.

Competition for survival contributes to an animal's biological success, as does its competition for mating partners; this is part of the "survival of the fittest" road of genetic development. Human competition in business and industry can produce more efficient systems and more reliable, affordable products and services. Sports, science, academics – they can all be advanced by competition.

But some competition is destructive. Competition that focuses on *artificial* or *short-term* gain can erode our opportunity to become financially independent. In "keeping up with the Joneses," you're on an endless path, with no place to eventually pull up and say, "Enough. I've arrived. I can stop chasing the rainbow." This is because the chase, not a concrete goal, has become the object. With no goal of your own in mind, the pursuit to overtake others has no limits. It will absorb all your effort – and all your money.

What's at work here? Who keeps us on this treadmill, this sometimes mad scramble for more, faster, new-and-improved? We do. We and the media-marketing wizardry that keeps pumping out the advertising and merchandizing campaigns for the best new widgets, the biggest new rainbows to chase. Then, like a gunfight in the Old West, it becomes an image showdown on the Main Street of our daily lives: who'll be the first to get the new carbon-Kevlar, lighter-than-air bicycle wheels? The satellite-powered cooking range? The full-buttocks tattoo? And if "Jones" gets it first, how can I catch up? This image saturation separates you from the real world, cocoons you in an artificial, media-story playtime. (We recently read up on a prescription drug to grow thicker eyelashes. Just $120! Scary.)

Again, we see that lethal mix of (a) surrendering your power (to the Joneses' choice of gas BBQs), (b) marketing genius (you *need* the latest and greatest), and (c) unhealthy reward training (with endorphin buzzes or fear impulses from the wrong things). Rather than just Madison Ave. swindling you, the spending trends of another person – a buddy from the gym, a neighbor, a coworker – are giving you the message that you're falling behind, that a penny saved is a chance wasted to own the hottest electric toothbrush-stereo-microwave combination (with Dolby-surround sound) south of the Arctic Circle.

What forces are at work here? There are several.

Because I Deserve It

"You don't get what you deserve; you get what you negotiate" is one of the glib mottoes in business management. Sounds harsh, but there is a critical truth in it. A company will deal again and again with the same customers, suppliers, and so on, so integrity in negotiations today affects success in negotiations tomorrow. Short-term means nothing. You deserve consistently good results only if you can consistently negotiate them.

This is as true in our individual lives as it is in business: Long-term, you get what you work for, and that's what you deserve. If you want financial security, it's not a sprint but a marathon. Be thoughtful and discriminating not only in *what* you buy but in *why you buy it.* But there has been an overwhelming push in the corporate merchandizing world to convince you that, no matter the *value* or the *cost,* you *"deserve"* their products and services if you can draw breath and you have a buck to spend. Where did this enormously influential pattern in advertizing come from?

About forty years ago a shampoo company took a bold step in this arena. They signed up for a high-profile TV and print-media ad campaign that said, "Yes, our product costs more, but you're worth it." They didn't even attempt to say, "We cost more because we're better, so if you want better, buy us." They just equated a more expensive product with privilege or, more to the point, *entitlement*.   Spend more money as a statement of status – even if there's no relationship to value. This was, in many ways, a forecast of how the essence of consumption trends would soon be defined: "Perception = reality; actual value is secondary – *and that's okay."* The campaign was, and continues to be, a huge success.

This created a cosmic shift. Status had always been a factor in the market place – Elm Street wasn't Park Avenue, and a Ford was never going to be a Cadillac. There was a quiet, accepted perception: "You get what you pay for" (snake oils aside). Pricing, status, and quality went together, at least roughly. The shampoo campaign kicked all that in the butt, very loudly, and very publicly – "Ignore value, buy desire." Goodbye, Great Depression, Post-War Years, and Age of Aquarius. Hello, ConsumoRama. "Buy our product because it costs more and you deserve expensive things" – *that* was the message. Using a fashion industry analogy, self-indulgence became the "new black."*

Today we are deluged with the straight-out or deftly hidden message, "Forget the natural value or actual need

---

**For those who might view the shampoo maker as a benign maverick simply filling a hip demand: it is the oldest and largest firm in the cosmetics world, representing 500 brands and thousands of products. Their iconoclastic marketing opened Pandora's (Plastic) Box. If you doubt its influence, do a Web search for "You deserve it." More corporate commen-*

for this product. Buy it because you have the money (or the credit card), and owning or using it will prove to you – *and the Joneses* – that you're special." Now the advertizing monster wants to convince me *I'm special?* But wait a minute. They're selling this product to the whole world, to everyone – well, everyone who has the cash or credit card. Does that mean everyone is special, everyone "deserves" the warm radiance of lusher, thicker, bouncier hair that makes people turn their heads when we twirl around on a New York street corner like a magazine fashion model? Oh, please.

When we examine unsuccessful behavior in adult humans, we find much of it is actually childlike. Children generally are not worried about the future. They rely on their parents and family to nurture them and to provide avenues so the future looks promising, not threatening. Marketers exploit this childlike reliance on someone else's guidance and decisions through advertising on a dozen levels – direct, subliminal, associative, and so on – and through dozens of avenues – television, newspaper, Internet, movies, branding, direct mail, telemarketing, and so on. They strive for the

tary: this company bought out a global chain of "alternative" cosmetics stores and, according to some sources, dropped that firm's policy against animal testing, using the defense that a human's right to beauty superseded animals' rights to health. "I'm worth it; the hell with the dogs and monkeys."

reawakening and control of our comforting childlike attachment to being free from the responsibility of decisions. The aim of the marketing world is to open up those avenues and keep them open so the merchandisers can make our decisions for us. That's called paternalism. (As you may have gathered, we don't like it.)

We're being force-fed the images and visions of corporate marketing's media machine. If they can dictate our vision, they can dictate our endorphins. The agencies are spending billions appealing to your inner child, to convince you that you *do* "deserve" the newest soda pop, the latest tanning lotion, the biggest-baddest SUV, and the six-day glamour cruise to Jamaica. Well, hell, everyone needs a vacation, some refreshment, a car, and protection from the sun. These things might really *be* right for you, may fit into your goals and budget, and bring you real gratification. You shouldn't deny yourself what you earn, what you need, and what fits your plan. Just *have* a plan, and stick to it. If you do, you'll reach your goals. And you *will* deserve it.

But if you buy into all this hype, you're in for a load of trouble. Say goodbye to what was supposed to be your future ability to live well and be secure. This is the *Battle of the Titans*, the fundamental clash of you, the *Goal-Oriented Achiever* on a White Charger protecting your financial tomorrow, and the pillaging *Corporate Huckster* and his *Forces of Evil* promising you happiness today if you buy shampoo and flash-looking basketball shoes – and whatever else they're selling on the other one hundred sixteen TV channels.

The Warhol Dictum

"In the future, everyone will be world-famous for fifteen minutes." Andy Warhol first said this in the late 1960s, and then revisited it in 1979. The "You're worth it" shampoo campaign came in the middle. Why is that relevant? What has one got to do with the other? First, Warhol was right – and the shampoo ads were right. Not in truth, but in *perception,* and perception would *become* reality. How? Through marketing and media. Sure, 99.9999% of people would never truly *be* world-famous, a'la' Warhol.

But intensified consumer marketing and an invasive, evolving media worked to manipulate everyone's self-image, to carry Warhol's message into our subconscious. Together they fed our desires and created the inkling that maybe, just maybe, we *could* be world-famous. I *could* be a celebrity, or at least *close,* if I wear my hair like P. Diddy or Justin T. Or if I buy jeans like Heidi K. Or if I drink and eat and drive and fly like a thousand real celebs on TV and magazines and in the movies. I might not actually *be* world-famous, but I can buy the opportunity to pretend, and I can hang out with people who buy the same opportunities. With the media so *wired,* and the marketers so *ready,* can't we all play dress-up and join in the masquerade. Sure—if you want to pay price.

Entitlement

These changes gave birth, in many quarters, to a new belief in entitlement. Not the political football of welfare, educational programs, or other social services "entitlement," but *consumer-indulgence* entitlement, the sense that the individual has an elevated standing or delicacy or esteem or status by which he or she is entitled to special material rewards or luxuries or services, an entitlement that sets him or her apart from the Great Unwashed.

This touches on one of the authors' least-favorite words: empowerment. It has become a fashionable word because it seems to give the recipient the very thing we are so big on: power. But too often *empowerment* is a masquerade that institutions use to get people to do what they – the ad agency, the government bureaucracy, and so on, – want. The organization figures out what's best for itself and then, through "restructuring," merchandising, marketing, and so forth, convinces the populace that they are being "empowered" with some new choice, options, or opportunity. In fact, what they are being offered is something that meets the organization's goals but is packaged to appear to be of great benefit to saps like us. This glowing so-called opportunity sometimes goes under the term "entitlement." It is another corporate slap in the face of our self-respect.

Much of high-end (read "luxury") marketing and its wasteful consumption is founded on this state of mind, this emotional dependency on material self-reward. This is evident in the subliminal insinuation of the "you deserve it" campaign. This pitch says, "You've been a good boy, so you get a reward," the longed-for message from our childhoods. It appeals to insecure people. It's how you train a dog to fetch a stick. Our readers are above this, and we want them to recognize it. (Psychotherapist Benjamin Fry, from a BBC-TV program on "spending therapy," says "People overspend because they've got a low sense of self worth. If you feel very small on the inside and present yourself as very big on the outside, it's compensation.")

Okay. Enough moralizing, enough preaching sociologic ideologies about human character and the demise of the fiber that "made this country great." That's not the aim of this book. Our focus is on money – money, money, money, money, money – and the benefit that enough of it, salted away, makes one secure in the future. So our message once again is: Understand what motivates you. Recognize how endorphins work in your choice of options. Relate your choices to your goals. Keep your eyes on the prize. Prioritize well, balancing the desire for enjoyment today with your needs for the future. When it comes to spending – Think!

Another little story caught our attention as we were closing in on our deadline for this book, and we want to include it. But where? It could fit in The Slow Leak or Push-Button Spending or I Deserve It. It is certainly part of a skilled merchandiser's method to extract every possible dollar out of his/her target purchaser.

One of our nephews bought a large, popular American motorcycle (nameless for our purposes). It cost about $12,000 – a great deal of money, but not huge as new, large motorcycles go. Here's the hook: it is a very basic bike, and most of the fittings and options are functional, but only just. The merchandisers of this bike have gone to huge effort to create a cult or subculture around this bike, one of the key elements of which is that "your" bike should always be different from his/her bike.

Of course, you can spend $25,000 right out of the gate for one of the supremo models, and then customize that, but for those who can't convince their Significant Other or bank manager that 25Gs is available for a John-Travolta-look-alike two-wheeler, they can get in at half the Big Bucks amount, and be bled for the rest over two or three years.

In order to feed this very market that they helped artificially create, the dealers sell this range of very bland basic bikes at comparatively modest cost, and then pump up a huge after-market accessories supply chain. This way you can spend tens, hundreds, and thousands of dollars buying all the stuff that your friends and co-cycle-religionists don't have on their bikes. The potential additional revenue to the manufacturers is as high as popularity, marketing, and enthralled imagination can drive it.

This is the "Barbie Doll" model for motorcycle sales. The basic bike is your starter kit. No one really expects you to ride that tinny, back-of-the-showroom model up to the friendly canyon tavern for a brew with Huge Harry and the Brawny Bikers. First you have to get a high-volume air-cleaner with the chrome-plated band; next is the better handlebars – 16 types; then the shifter mods, from which you have six or eight to choose; finally, the catalog-custom exhaust (12 versions of headers and 20 versions of tailpipes, for 240 possible combinations, to avoid offending Huge Harry by duplicating *his* set-up). Don't sleep (or save any spare change) until your 'cycle is able to hold its head up as a paragon of fashion and accessorization.

What evidence supports our report? How did we discover this charming little finagle? We found the nephew's parts catalog on his coffee table – 1068 pages, maybe 20-40 items per page, ranging in price from ten dollars for a logo head-scarf to many thousands of dollars for transmission re-tooling kits. And this wasn't the *manufacturer's* catalog, just one of many that supply after-market accessories for these bikes.

A clever scheme, no? Get the buyer into a low-level, untrendy machine for $10-12,000, one that gains him entry to the periphery of a "club," a club that conforms by "spending large" to be different from fellow members. The bike just becomes an avenue for competing with the Joneses (or with Huge Harry.)

Contentment, and Its Absence

Do social and community attitudes play a role in our financial future? Is there something constructive to be gained by discussing social philosophy and personal ethics in a book about money management? Yes. The entire point of this book is to help people be happier, now and in the future. Part of that happiness will come from a sense of security that a healthy bank balance brings. But in building that balance one makes thousands of choices, challenging decisions that must mesh not only with one's financial goals, but with one's values, one's social and personal attitudes, as well.

Further, if we are successful with this book, we will influence, to a degree, the values of thousands of people. So the authors have a responsibility to pass along what we think are conscientious personal and social viewpoints about the topics in this book.

Four hundred years ago, John Donne wrote "No man is an island, entire of itself." Almost everything we do involves other people, often in situations we revisit repeatedly. What we think "we deserve" is not as meaningful as the value and benefits we construct for ourselves in our constant interaction with others. If we ignore this, we risk leading a life of isolation. Losing sight of the value of others boxes one into a life solely based on that individual's views and ability to fend for himself or herself.

What we deserve to receive as individuals in a society should be based on what contribution we make to that society, and on what value the society places on us. The fact that too often this doesn't happen, because of the failings or selfishness of some, doesn't change that principle. To decide for myself what I deserve, on the basis of my own singular view of myself, is to divorce myself from the values of society, from my community. And then, separated from my community, I am alone, with a long, unpleasant, and sometimes never-ending road back.

This is not to say we must go to the other extreme, not think for ourselves, and let society dictate to us who and what we are. Some aspects of society are as flawed, as corrupt, as the worst commercial motives of the merchandisers; in fact, they sometimes join forces, intentionally or by accident. We support those values that are constructive to a healthy community, that represent security and advancement for its members. We *must* maintain individuality for our own well-being and unique rewards, but as integrated parts of our communities.

In planning this chapter, we came across one of our favorite sayings about individual imagination and achievement, the opposite of media-and-marketing-control and widespread conformity. It's worth reflecting on when you catch yourself falling down: "Only people who are mediocre can be at their best all the time."

PATH FIVE

"Rigidity Equals Strength"

Across the spectrum of the Seven Paths, some ideas are more practical and applied, for instance the "slow leak," and some, like power, focus on attitude and psychology. In this, the Fifth Path, our discussion begins with the psychological side and then branches into the practical.

A dialogue on the risks of *inflexibility,* the resistance to constructive change, could fit anywhere in a book on human behavior – first, last, or in the middle. Since it's opposite, agility of mind and perspective, is a vital benefit on the road to success, introducing the struggle between rigidity and flexibility here, reflecting back on the four preceding paths as well as forward to the final two, should give the reader another valuable tool in understanding the psychology of money and its roles in life.

Set-in-concrete attitudes can result in debt as a life-style (I've always used that product; I don't care what it costs), lost opportunities (I'd never live in that town no matter how good the job is), all your eggs in one basket

(It's a sure thing; he's been my broker for years), dangerous associations (Known her since grade school! I'd never say no to her), hubris (I can't be wrong again!), and a failure to challenge your own assumptions.

A rigid mind-set is the best device for freezing out options, and a formula for certain disaster in an uncertain world. In solving problems, blocking options at the outset (being rigid) runs the risk of missing the best, or at least better, answers. At the same time, having no criteria at all for rejecting options (being sloppy) invites disorder. Humans often get caught in this dilemma and let themselves be forced too far in one direction (too few choices) or too far in the other (chaos).

So why do we have a chapter devoted to rigidity but not to sloppiness? Actually, nearly all the other chapters do address sloppiness in its many forms: mental, emotional, lifestyle, practical, and so on. This can lead to a sense that money management needs nothing but rigid and unyielding discipline, but this isn't true. Flexibility is one of the most rewarding skills to have in any venture, especially financial, and its absence often leads to rapid monetary decline.

Pleasure Centers

As we might expect, brain chemistry and mental function have a lot to do with how a rigid mind-set interferes with wealth-building. If we feel more rewarded by sticking to a set of concrete rules than by regular small triumphs in our financial goals, that's because we learned somewhere that rules are more valuable than goals, and our brain responds accordingly, reinforcing one and not the other. In this case, the adherence to an unyielding code produces less fear reaction in the amygdala and more endorphins in the pleasure centers than it would from reaching the financial goal. We are not born with these responses, only the ability to learn them – and the ability to retrain them.

In the very real, practical world that this book is aimed at, the authors' job is to aid readers in unwinding rigidly held beliefs that might be obstructing them from reaching, for example, their savings targets. To do this, we will probe into all sorts of juicy parts of the personality and outlook, "pointing fingers and naming names," as they say.

Rigidity in beliefs and in practice comes largely from a sense, perhaps a fear, that to wander from the fixed code, to take a risk in method or thinking, is to invite mistakes, which will invite weakness, which will invite tragedy and disaster. Indeed, mistakes will happen in the real world, and weaknesses will be revealed. We would argue that it's better to make the mistake and reveal the weakness with your head up and eyes open, and take steps to reverse the weakness, than to have the weakness catch you unawares and cause a major problem. There is no perfect answer to this argument, but it's one that everyone should consider as they makes their plans and evaluate their progress in life.

Hardness of the Head

If we return to the themes that precede this chapter, we see a thousand illustrations of how rigidity as opposed to agility would affect the course of your actions and your life. Let's focus on some major points to illustrate how the reader can benefit from these comparisons.

You might begin with a monthly savings goal that's too ambitious, but you stick to it rigidly. That can do a lot of damage as you punish yourself psychologically for "falling short." This can also hurt your resolve to follow through with other goals as you deal with the frustrations you perceive as failure. Give yourself a break. Back off on the goal by 20% or 30% and reevaluate your plans. If that goes well, try adding 5% after three or four months. Be flexible.

Your core personal values are extremely important in developing a plan for your life that's going to be inwardly rewarding; but rigidly worshiping all those values all the time, and expecting those close to you to do so also, can be suffocating for you and others, and can strangle your ability to survive and prosper. So be a little flexible in how you apply those values at least some of the time; even test the validity of those values if they seem to be too great an obstacle to your goals.

We all know people who are "control freaks," who try to monopolize every ounce of power in the room. Protecting your personal power is important, even vital, but you have friends and family who actually do have your best interests at heart, and you can release some of your power to them. You have to protect yourself from con men and women, from the pyramid and Ponzi wizards of the world, and from dozens of other types who mean you no good. But there will be many genuine situations in money, in business, and in life where you will benefit from sharing your power. Be careful, but don't be rigid.

The Rats in the Bread Box

To illustrate some of the pitfalls of rigidity in the real-money world, many people who put their money into "investments" lose it because the investors *are* rigid; they're too inflexible in their ties to XYZ Securities and networks of so-called friends and institutions. Locked in self-justification, these mini-financiers, some of them very seasoned, may refuse to accept that they and their circle might be getting fleeced. They become frozen to their assumptions and beliefs, and to their pride in their original decisions, without the humility and flexibility to ask if they are, perhaps, making any mistakes.

The names of investment shysters in the head-lines yesterday, today, and tomorrow will just be the latest in an unending string of history's often-white collar bunko artists. California, the authors' home state, has seen more than its share, in every stripe from small-town, back-slapping, feel-good flim-flammers, right through to City of Angels gurus and demi-goddesses who are simply too exalted to be questioned by the Great

Unwashed. From their perches they prey on the rest of us if we give them an opening.

In many of these cases, a cult of personality develops around the "leader" – he or she can do no wrong. Perhaps a paternal (or maternal) aura evolves around the crook(s). People adopt him or her as a financial role model because of all the signs of wealth around. Frequently the investors are linked to the leader and each other by religion or an ideology.

The records show that, especially when times are good, these schemes pull in hundreds of millions, up to billions, of dollars, fueled too often by poorly informed but well-funded, trusting citizens who just don't see the signs of deception until they're in so deep they refuse to believe the obvious. Then, when the heady times of ready cash begin to fade, the houses of cards collapse and the rats run for cover. The Great Recession of 2008-09 flushed many of these out of the woodwork. (We'd like to name names, but people like this find ways of getting revenge.)

We've seen prison terms of six, eight, up to seventy-five years, but these sentences didn't get the investors their money back. Why did they get fleeced? Too often it's a matter of *pride* and a *fear of being wrong*. There is almost always a point where the scheme shows signs of collapsing before it does, but people say, "I haven't made a mistake. This will all be okay in the end. In fact, to prove I'm right, I'm going to put more money into the venture." People let rigidity of perspective blind them to the truth and miss any chance to get out before it all goes down the gurgler.

The $60 "Trust" Fund

If we've preached a mantra, if we've been rigid ourselves in what we've said, it's to always *THINK* about how you manage your money, how you spend it, and how you make decisions about your financial welfare. While we stick to that, we have a "non-rigidity" clause in the contract, too. One of the wisest small-money decisions we have encountered in our town came from Tim and Collette, a middle-income couple who moved out here from Iowa a long time ago. We noticed they lived comfortably and happily, within their means, and that concern about marital finances rarely entered their conversations.

By happenstance one day we found out what might have been the key to that. They had an agreement that they'd never argue over anything less than $60. Either of them could spend $60 and not have any questions asked about it by the other. Sixty dollars wasn't the point. It was the contract of trust the agreement represented. They both knew they had the *flexibility* to spend sixty dollars any time. That built and cemented, over time, a bond of financial trust. With that, they both knew the spouse "had my back" when it came to money. So they relaxed about it.

Rigidity can also present itself as biases. A fixation on a particular product or service or location, or against another one, may limit flexibility in shopping for a better price. Gender and subculture bias can do the same, or much worse. Unfounded biases about geographical locations or schools or vacation spots or a hundred other things can also lock one into spending more than is necessary or even satisfying, and they even interfere with job prospects. Again, fear, endorphins, and neuroeconomics play their roles to some degree when someone acts out a bias in any of these things. Only by being flexible and growing from our experiences can we change those brain responses.

Making it Personal

We'd like to give you some practical "war game" lessons in how rigidity can limit your success. This will expand somewhat beyond the scope of this book – saving and spending – into a discussion that touches on investing, but we think there is some value for the reader in throwing more light on the effects of rigidity.

The battle for success in life – in any area of life – will involve *tactics* and *principles.* Successful people typically have core principles, and they stick with them devotedly (perhaps rigidly!), as the faithful follow the Ten Commandments or the tenets of Buddhism. In the context of this book, it could be that one's principles would be to *keep* the teachings of Guidepost 1 and 2 and *avoid* the Paths to Poverty. Tactics, then, are the behaviors or methods people follow to implement their principles.

The famous (and super-wealthy) investment manager Warren Buffet has a core principle – to make a profit for his investors. He pursues that principle with the tactic "buy low, sell high." However, tactics and principles can become muddled, with a very negative outcome. Asked how long he liked to keep a stock, Buffett said, "Forever." This answer distorted his principle—to make a profit—and his tactic of buying low and selling high. How, and what bad outcome did this cause?

Buffett's firm bought Coca Cola at around $10 a share, which, over many years, rose eight times higher. No asset goes up forever, so Buffett keeping a stock "forever" forces *rigidity* on his tactic (buy low, sell high), compromising his principle (make a profit). In this case, the "buy low, sell high" tactic was squeezed by the *pseudo*-principle, "hold forever." Coca Cola dropped by over half and has never come close to its former high. Buffett is one of history's great investors, but even Mr. Big can slip up by being *too rigid.*

Principles define the core beliefs that generally govern the direction of one's life, and they need to be firm, if not quite rigid. But tactics require *flexibility* within these overarching principles. A principle may turn you away from gambling, cigarette, or alcohol stocks, but, outside of areas defined by principles as off-limits, you execute the tactics that exploit the current environment.

When daily tactics are replaced by rigid principles, this leads to weakness, not strength. Principles create a life of healthy constraints combined with stability, but applying the constraints must remain flexible so daily life can adapt within those limits. An example is working hard when you're young so you don't have to work so hard when you're old (defined as over 85). It includes being opportunity-ready. When attractive opportunities appear, you need to be flexible enough to seize them – *carpe diem* – perhaps overriding your principle to always do time-consuming research.

You need to challenge your assumptions and remain flexible. You need to prepare intellectually and academically for the future, so you maximize your options. You need to think ahead in a tactical sense about what might happen, how you might respond, and how this might affect your family and friends. Many great disasters have occurred when people confused tactics with principles (and failed to realize that others might not to do the same). Custer may have felt a need to express America's vaunted *principle* of manifest destiny against the certain *tactical* odds of the 7th Cavalry getting annihilated at the Little Bighorn; Sitting Bull knew the score. Did the "unsinkable" Titanic use navigation *tactics* in North Atlantic sea lanes that violated the *principle* of avoiding icebergs at night? Millions of investors make money in the stock market every day by applying their tactics to their principles, while the same numbers lose by confusing the two.

Jeffrey Skinner, a consulting actuary for fifty years and president of Southland Pension Services gave us another story. A client heard that he could borrow from this pension plan to pay his credit card debt. Jeff said he could, but that money in a pension plan is protected from bankruptcy; other assets are not. Jeff suggested he leave his pension plan alone and learn to control his credit card spending. The client knew better: he legally borrowed from the pension plan, paid his credit card debt, continued to spend, and went bankrupt. He lost the pension plan dollars he'd taken out; if he'd listened to Jeff, they would still be in his plan, protected from the courts, lawyers, etc.

In summary, rigidity does not mean strength, but fear and weakness. The world is constantly shifting. You can't know all the changes beforehand. Be ready to change directions when tactical conditions change. Roger Fisher in *Getting To Yes* explains that understanding your interests and how to achieve them is far more successful than focusing on a tactic or fixed position. Learn the landscape, not just one way to traverse it. Don't be driven by ideology and inflexible beliefs, but by consistency in goals. In matters not to do with morals and ethics, the end justifies the means, so be pragmatic.

PATH SIX

Relationships, and How 2 - 1 can = ½

This chapter attempts to bring the practical considera-
tions of personal relationships, good ones and bad ones,
into the financial security picture.   Seat-of-the-pants
planning and execution in relationships can bring on
monetary disaster. Though we discuss marriage, per se,
the advice refers to any relationship in which the
partners share in the financial whole.

Money and love – both are resources that benefit
someone best when invested well, and, over the ages,
each has been the cause of delicious joy and shattering
heartbreak. Is one more important than the other? If
you doubt that love is more valuable than money,
compare a wealthy but emotionally empty marriage with
an emotionally strong marriage of modest means. The
first one may be more colorful, but the second one
brings both people more happiness. However, if you
think money is unimportant in a relationship, remember
that love alone won't feed you, clothe you, or educate
you and your children. The daily mechanics of living

require the nuts and bolts of fiscal supply.   Dough.
Bread. Moolah. Scratch.

Most good advice about money also applies to
emotions.   When both are in good health, you can be
generous with either.   But when one of them is showing
signs of distress, it's time to reduce your risks, or to
"keep your powder dry."   This is *at least* as true with
your heart as with your wallet, because many people
find it's easier to recover from an economic setback than
an emotional one.   Regrettably, a poorly planned
relationship can set you up for both, and the poverty that
may result is rarely just financial.

Let's look closer.

Marriage and Divorce

A relationship typically begins with passion, but the
marriage that might ensue is actually an agreement –
personal, practical, and economic – with inevitable and
forceful connections between the emotional and
practical sides of that contract (and its all-too-frequent
sequel, divorce). Inseparable from this discussion are:

1) spending choices and patterns in the heady and
   unpredictable world of courtship and romance as
   well as during the marriage years
2) what things constitute real value to the partners
3) media and marketing pressures in self-image and
   fiscal decisions
4) the emotions unleashed in money disagreements,

and as many more topics as there are marital agreements. In this section, we'll try to cover the ones most relevant to your financial interests.

Even though financial differences are among the greatest sources of marital misery, couples often don't discuss money and budgets before the wedding. They thrash out details of inspiring vacations, housing locations, and babies' names well before the wedding date. Why is finance neglected?

Do couples (and families?) avoid the topic to keep romance and harmony in the forefront of attention? Yes. Do they fear that talking about financial realities will be misinterpreted as a lack of trust? Yes. Do they see pre-nuptial agreements as a sign that breakups are more likely than imagined? Yes. Are there sound, rational reasons for reaching understandings on these things before marriage? Yes. Are there good sources in books, on the Web, and via professional advice to guide you and yours to rewarding outcomes on these points? Yes. Do all intelligent, squared-away couples go through this process before they tie the knot? NO! Why not? Because "Love Is Blind."

We're going to set the romantic niceties aside while we ask and answer some hard questions and investigate some messy subjects about love, lust, and money.

Families and Money

Financial values frequently pass on from parent to child. You can often tell much about a person's fiscal orientation by the family's example. Here is a range of financial attitudes that offspring might "inherit":

1. Cautious with money
2. Careless with money (numerous credit cards, gambling, unreasonable debt)
3. Money promised as a motivator and/or withheld as punishment
4. "Male and female spending patterns are incompatible."
5. Money as an entrepreneurial tool (good if employed wisely; possibly dangerous)
6. If provided freely, money is a curse, leading to waste and corruption (e.g., "trust fund kids")

In general, people do learn their basic views about money in the home, but this is a broad observation about behavior, not a concrete rule. Individuals grow and change; they develop good habits and lose bad ones – or the reverse. Many offspring from wealthy families find their way to money troubles, and some from meager means work their way to the penthouse suite. Season your perspectives on a possible mate with a grain of salt.

Credit history

In the Third Path we highlighted the sayings of notables from Socrates to P.T. Barnum. Here, in the Sixth Path, we offer the words of the great rock-and-roller, Bo Diddley: "You can't judge a book by its cover."

The worst surprise in a marriage can come from discovering the facts of a spouse's credit – or lack of it.

While crime and gambling, drugs and addiction, serial relationships and unexpected children may typically (though not always!) be known, credit history is often not revealed until after the wedding, when the two people are financial partners under the law. What may be hidden behind a respectable job, tasteful clothes, charming manner, and a luxury car? Appearances not only can be deceiving, they are often *intended* to be.

People who develop bad credit histories often build up these lifestyles gradually, creating an illusion, first to themselves, then to others, that they can *live high* on what they earn plus all the great things that are going to happen with their "new jobs" (that never happen) or new relationships (and self-inflicted delusions) or the big risks they've taken. And then, bang! the dreams wash out and they're deep in debt, living on credit, and trying to hide that fact from their bankers, employers, friends, and lovers. In the old days, 90% of these people were con-artists and grifters. But now lots of "straight" people end up this way because credit mechanisms allow it to happen to good people who simply lose control.

How can you clarify a potential mate's credit standing without crushing the romance? There are the "film noir" methods: a private eye, rifling files, questioning the neighbors. But theatrics aside, getting such information isn't easy. You may have to rely on gut feelings, a paper and pencil, and a few simple observations.

Make a realistic estimate of your intended's income; ask some simple questions, check job-search sources, and quiz your friends. Subtract income taxes. Add up his or her monthly expenses for food, rent, transportation, and general upkeep. Calculate any "extras" you can see: restaurants, entertainment, toys, vacations, home furnishings, luxury items. Finally, add in new purchases made regularly. Are the expenses exceeding the after-tax income? Is it even close? If so, be forewarned. There will be more expenses you don't see. Fiscal profiles like these often go hand-in-hand with credit and debt problems, unpaid personal loans, and even back taxes.

In the end, if you can't discover what you need to know (note, we said *need* to know), you may have to ask him or her directly in a polite and considerate way. Open a discussion about future financial planning, a home purchase, children's education, and so on. Suggest you both sit down together and put your income and expense figures on paper so you can see what your combined financial health will be. This meeting may resolve your concerns – or it might never happen. Then you'll have some decisions to make.

Differing Material Expectations

Both partners want a house, but he grew up cramped in a "shoebox" and now wants a mansion, while she grew up in a sprawling ranch-style and, instead, wants something efficient and compact. One sees a car as transportation, the other as a symbol of success or a thrilling ride on a country road. Spouse X sees stylish clothes as an investment and personal expression, while Spouse Y darns socks and loves finding old favorites on sale.

The examples of out-of-synch tastes and choices are endless. Perfectly coordinated minds are impossible, and who would want that, anyway? So how do you reach harmony?

Roger Fisher, internationally acclaimed director of the Harvard Negotiation Project and world leader in dispute settlement, has an answer, referred to as the "one-text" method. When two negotiators disagree at a basic level, both viewpoints usually can't be fulfilled. However, the parties can change their viewpoints and expectations as long as both see the changes in their best interests. In this way, they can both reach a happy outcome. How does this work?

Fisher uses a couple house-hunting as an example. Instead of both coming to the table with full-blown images of two different houses (two "texts"), the couple starts with a blank slate, i.e., no fixed plans for what each "must have." They flip a coin to see who starts, and then each partner in turn gets to add a room or feature to the house, with the other partner approving it on the spot or by negotiation. For example, spouse A wins the coin toss and elects an upstairs master bedroom with a mountain view. Spouse B agrees ("yes"), with a proviso that a home office, of what ever size and configuration, be on the same floor. (This isn't B's first priority, just a small condition added to A's first choice.) A agrees ("yes"). B's first choice is a library for study and to house their large book collection. A asks B to change the choice because many basic house features are more essential than a library, but agrees to B's concept ("yes"), proposing to include book and study space into the office B mentioned. This is fine with B ("yes"); B then makes an open-plan kitchen-dining area B's first choice. A agrees ("yes"), and then makes the next choice. B agrees and makes the next choice. They continue in this pattern to "build" their house.

This approach creates "one text." Both partners learn that, by working toward agreement (a series of "yes"s), they stand a better chance of getting their main desires approved. The practical limitations become their budget, the market, and city and zoning approval, not each other's disagreements. Each partner accepts that reaching a workable, negotiated agreement is more important than staying glued to a list of preconceived but one-sided choices.

This has proven an effective way to reach agreement on everything from international price disputes to getting the Russians to leave Afghanistan in 1989. We think it will work for you.

The Stork Arrives

Children are the unpredictable addition to marital finances today. For thousands of years, the *arrival* of a child was, within reason, predictable, though the *survival* wasn't. To balance short life expectancies with a reliance on child labor, primitive societies evolved high birth rates. Infant death, subsistence economies, and the absence of coast-to-coast orthodontics and pearl-handled MP3 players meant that the expected cost of raising children was known, and it was low. But today, even with trends of fewer children per family, the little devils keep showing up and disrupting family finances.

As our societies have become more complex, so have the questions about children and money. Will one or both partners work? Will the parents do all the child-rearing, or use outside help? Private school or public school? "Child labor": allowances; house work; chores; after-school jobs?

These don't even scratch the surface of the challenges for today's parents in America and other advanced countries. Some human endeavors and human dynamics in families don't change, but the accelerated evolution of the social, cultural, educational, and recreational aspects of a child's universe has made it ever more difficult for parents to keep up, putting a tremendous strain on a family's ability to budget for the cost of children.

Is there a single big secret that applies to kids and money? No. What we can say is that nearly everything in the book that has preceded this section *does* apply here – in spades. Goals, values, peers, motivation, power, shopping and spending disciplines, entitlement attitudes, flexibility – it all stacks up in this corner "to the max," as they say (used to say?). Kids require all the observation, perception, planning, acting, and endurance skills we have just to keep them in sight, much less to control the cost of keeping them alive – and human.

So, if you're planning on having kids, keep this book as a reference for the future. Buy two dozen. Give them as gifts to all the new parents you know. Take it to school and give it to the teachers. If you have young kids yourself, put this book in their Christmas stockings; teach them to read from it. On the other hand, if you have teenage kids . . . beat them with it. (We didn't say that!)

Budgets Big and Small

There is a saying in California: To make a small fortune in the wine business, start out with a large fortune. Unless you've done meticulous research and watch everything you spend, money simply disappears between pruning in the winter and harvest in the fall. By the time you're seeing any income, you may have already spent more than you'll ever earn back. Farm budgets are nice to look at, but nature can't read them, markets don't respect them, and some people can't stick to them.

Much the same applies to family budgets. The confidence a couple puts into their financial planning can seem pretty empty when a health crisis hits, the roof starts leaking, or what looked like a reliable retirement investment goes up in smoke. And that assumes the couple had been able to discuss a budget, agree on it, and stick to it before the set-back hit. But as bad as things can look when disaster bends the budget, they're a lot worse when there isn't one.

A household budget can stifle a relationship or make it work financially. If both partners don't agree on the numbers and the restraints, the whole concept can break a relationship rather than secure it. It can become a source of ongoing conflict and recrimination. However, a budget that is mutually constructed (think Fisher's "one-text" method), balances necessities with enjoyment, serves the outlooks of both partners, and advances the common goals of the couple can be a source of great strength and reward in the marriage.

It can be pretty simple. You start by making a list. The basic elements of survival are food, water, shelter, and warmth. So your early list can be:

1. groceries
2. rent or mortgage
3. utilities
4. clothes

Both spouses need to agree on the list. Use "one-text" if you must. Also, if you live in the tropics and like to go naked, "clothes" can be moved down the list. If self-determined transportation (what most people call "driving") is important to your survival, then write in "car" (or scooter, bicycle, or Norton Commando). And so on.

Once your "Basic Needs" list is complete, don't add anything else. Get out your paper, pencil, and calculator. Write down your total household monthly income, minus taxes and any expenses you have (e.g., student loans, previous divorce, national debt of Sri Lanka). Now subtract a realistic amount for food, rent, and utilities every month. Depending on your situation, a car or clothes might be next, or insurance (house; car), or education costs, or some other expense(s) that is tied to your essential needs, security, and/or goals.

Are you now allowed to write in "vacation, entertainment, 'War-Games-on-Wall Street Options-trading Software'?" No. Why? After your safety and survival are accounted for, refer back to Path Two – and put something into your savings account. Your savings are part of your survival, part of your security, and part of your goals.

Okay, so once you have *really* covered all the basics, including savings, you can begin, by mutual agreement, to bring in other expenses. We don't have to go through all the lessons all over again from previous chapters, do we? Lessons about healthy self-esteem and self-image, the media, Madison Avenue, phony entitlement, surrendering your power, low-value consumption? No, we didn't think so.

So, every month, all the essentials get paid first, something goes into your savings, and only then do you indulge your desires – material desires, that is.

Jumping the Gun and the Genius of Youth

Don't think this is all you need to know about relationships and money. We've just got you started on the topic, but we've covered the key elements. Here are a few more ugly truths along this Path to Poverty.

Yes, your parents were incredibly lucky to survive until you reached Age 16 and could tell them how the universe really works. How did they get that far without you? Well, youth is good for the speed and agility to hit the slider low and away, and for cracking the books on an all-nighter for tomorrow's chemistry exam after a 36-

hour stint on your favorite social networking site with your truly best friend studying abroad in Rawalpindi. Youth is *not* experienced in long-term commitments. One of the biggest financial mistakes a person can make is to use the passion and optimism of youth as a marriage counselor.

Early Mistakes

Early marriage is usually a big mistake. It compounds all of the other relationship money problems we've mentioned above (remember, this book is about *money)*, makes "due diligence" prior to tying the knot impossible, and magnifies the risk of divorce. The partners have no credit history and little notion of how money is used and shared. Money can become a proxy for love or attention and lead to excess shopping, excess frugality, or an inability to compromise when funds are short. We could harangue you with more examples, and it's probably grossly unsafe of us to say this, but: "Take our word for it."

What's worse than marrying too young? Having kids too young. Children change the goals and dynamics of everything about the relationship, and rightly so. But when they come early in a marriage, much of the groundwork a couple hoped to establish while they still had freedom, flexibility, and "selfish" direction may get long-delayed or never accomplished. Early children bring new costs just when parents have lower earning potential. This strains funds for housing, food, education, and so forth. This can all lead to disappointment, friction, neglect, abuse, and divorce. Children are wonderful additions to the universe. Plan them well.

How young is too young to marry? Hard to say, but let's take a crack at it. You've finished your formal education and see a clear career or other journey ahead. You're driven by a passion to succeed, have the framework for a reliable financial plan for the first three years, and you see yourself and your partner together for life, so . . . wait another year.

But that's a glib answer. The facts are these (from William Galston, Ph.D., a Presidential advisor and expert on family life in America): if you graduate from high school, wait until you're over twenty to have children, and get married before having children, you only have an 8% chance of living in poverty. Poverty is almost guaranteed if you fail to do these three things.

The Reality of Divorce: $2 - 1 = \frac{1}{2}$

Everyone knows the horror stories of divorce. One partner or the other, if not both, recounts the trials and tribulations of the marriage, the sins of the spouse, the accusations and allegations, and, perhaps, the "relief at being free." Even more frequent are the financial woes: alimony paid or unpaid, child support paid or unpaid, the budgetary strain of two households, and the huge set-back in material security of both exes. (While divorces of wealthy couples may not impoverish the pair, it's certain that the lawyers' fees reduce everyone's piece of the pie. For this discussion we're using a middle-income reference.)

The financial details can be infinite, but the divided assets and divorced couple's incomes are not. The investment pool, if there is one, gets divided and often distressed. Two households, both compromised, will emerge and virtually every domestic expense increases, some by 100% or more. Children develop extra needs. New and expensive social lives and new personal expenses may evolve to explore new relationship options. Another marriage may lead to another family, all sharing a finite income. More expensive medical care may ensue, as married people tend to spend less on healthcare. Legal expenses may linger and recur. For these reasons and more, we created the Divorce Equation: $2 - 1 = \frac{1}{2}$.

Is divorce, or any similar division of domestic assets, a path to financial hardship? Yes, and not just for the parents. Most children of divorce live with one parent, so parenting is not efficiently shared. There tend to be fewer educational opportunities for the kids. Childcare costs rise, directly to an agency or sitter, or because the "home parent" works less. Both parents save less, work later in life, and retire at an older age. It isn't much fun.

Getting relationships right is damned difficult. This chapter should help.

PATH SEVEN

Going to The Dark Side

Just as we all stick the nastiest chores at the bottom of our to-do lists, hoping they'll somehow go away, we "saved" this section until the end because it dwells on bad choices regarding money. Oh, not purse-snatching, armed robbery, or stealing from the collection basket, but actions, even whole lifestyles, that erode one's fiscal direction and self-esteem. These choices can have ethical, even moral, implications in the minds of some, but our theme here is your money, not your soul.

As you read the following pages, it's important to keep some themes and concepts in mind that we introduced early and have gone back to time and again:

1. With steady savings and a long time-horizon, almost everyone in America can become a millionaire

2. Off-balance emotions, the subconscious, and brain chemistry can derail your financial journey even faster than conscious choices

3. Persistent small leaks will always slow down
    your financial bicycle
4. Outside forces are a constant challenge to your
    savings discipline
5. Goals that dovetail with your personal values
    bring huge personal power to the decisions you
    make on the journey.

Point 1, a long time-horizon, can't be over-emphasized. Compound interest, multiplying your investments for twenty or thirty years, can make you rich; but that interest can break you if it's mounting up on your credit card debt. Likewise, good lessons learned early create the most benefit over time, while harmful choices at an early age multiply the damage in the years to come.

In addressing the following activities we risk making an enemy of the very reader this chapter is meant to help. These behaviors are often described by society as being illicit, illegal, immoral, self-indulgent – ethical or moral misconduct. Is asking the reader to own up to one (or more) like asking him to admit to Original Sin? No, it's the bank accounts we're interested in, not Eternal Damnation.

While it is an obvious and widespread malady, and the potential cause of major financial pain, misuse of alcohol doesn't make an appearance here, primarily because it's gotten so much coverage in so many other channels. But we recognize that it can be a huge problem for individuals and families, and that it has caused untold disasters in the lives of millions of young people, too.

Bob's Bookie

We'll call him Bob. Once a patient of Lance Mason's, Bob showed some common human failings. When Oscar Wilde said, "I can resist anything but temptation," he expressed a kinship with Bob and his shaky self-discipline. The Groucho Marx quip "I'd never belong to a club that would have me as a member" fit Bob and his low self-esteem.

At every appointment, Bob would detour into the private consulting room to make a short phone call. He would ask politely, duck in, make his call, and duck out. Sometimes he also made the calls as he was leaving. Bob worked in TV and communications and traveled from another city to the practice, so the calls seemed important, but for some reason he didn't make them from his cell phone. When Dr. Mason finally asked him what the calls were about, Bob sheepishly admitted they were to a sports-betting agency. Who knows how many calls he made day-in, day-out through the week? Or through the year? His embarrassment at discussing this was a clear sign of Bob's failing personal willpower and self-esteem.

What would you find if you wired Bob to a brain scanner and, as he figured his chances of winning, losing, or being discovered, you recorded his endorphin readings and fear signals? If you charted the results and compared them to his bank statements, you'd no doubt learn a lot about Bob's likelihood of ever finding security. Several *basic* things are clear about Bob: his is not a predictable method of goal-pursuit, he isn't learning much about himself that's constructive, and he's not using his personal power to control the direction of his finances. By now, you know a dozen ways to illustrate these facts.

Unfortunately, a sports bookie is one of many avenues along *The Dark Side's* path to poverty, each of them leading the dream of future wealth to a tragic dead-end. These patterns can start when you're young, and some can take you places where financial U-turns are painfully difficult. While a few examples might seem too crass for most of our readers to be drawn to, some are as everyday as buying a daily lotto ticket.

Happy Days

Reefer, weed, ganja, hash, coke, blow, whiff, X, XTC, smack, horse, speed – you get the idea. We have seen no correlation for investors between getting high and getting rich, but if one of our readers can explain how buying and using any of these will contribute to the goal of monetary security for the user (rather than the dealer), we are prepared to listen to the arguments. Seriously, drugs at any age – and we're not going to argue over addictive, non-addictive, and so on. – are not going to increase your ability to fund your kids' schooling, the remodel of your house, or vacations in Portugal and New Zealand. The only holiday you might get is a long one in the Graybar Hotel.

You don't need us to tell you that cash spent on "the habit" is money down a rat-hole – it's its own path to poverty. If you haven't started, don't. If you have and you can walk away, do so. If you can't walk away, get help. Advice on drug dependence on any level is outside our envelope, but family and professional help is your best route home.

School's Out

The world loves the story of the underdog who left school at sixteen, is now CEO of Maxitron, the intergalactic leader in auto upholstery services, and has no money problems. We love those stories, too, but they're scarce. Don't bet your life on one, and don't just take our word for it. Look around. Nearly everyone who drops out of school finds every aspect of his or her financial life harder: getting a job, keeping it, pay scales, buying a home, having a family, *saving cash.* There are exceptions. A good marriage, hard work, frugal living, careful saving – these things can bring you a secure and even comfortable life in America, even without a high school diploma. But those successes are rare, difficult, and usually tied to a lot of luck.

We don't belittle the person who doesn't have the chance at education. Both of our fathers grew up poor and left school very young. We admire and respect people who overcome these backgrounds. But they will be the first to tell you how much easier putting cash in the bank would have been if they'd had a better education.

Dropping out is a ticket to the School of Hard Knocks, so if you did, and want back in, there are a hundred ways to do it. You can start by <u>knocking</u> – on a principal's door – and asking some questions. The school will help you. If you hit a dead end, contact us through our website, www.sevenpathstopoverty.com. Schools are things we know about.

Gambling

Life is full of risks. All investments have risks, as we all know, and bigger risks offer bigger rewards, as long as the "game" isn't rigged. We will often sign up for risks to get the rewards on offer. The way to play this game is to always take the bets that have better than 50-50 odds, and then use legal, legitimate ways to try to improve those odds. Over the long haul, if you always take the options with a better than 50-50 chance, you'll win.

Risk-taking, however, isn't the same as gambling. Gambling is throwing money at games in which the odds are ALWAYS, repeat *always,* against you. In gambling, you never have a 50-50 chance. Do it long enough and you will lose. Play for a lot and you will lose a lot. This is old news to gamblers. Again, look around a casino – losers everywhere. Casino landscapes are not reality. Can you honestly tell yourself that you've got more than a snowball's chance in Hell of getting rich by gambling?

(Another gem from Bill Paulin, Ph.D.: "I spent a day with the VP of Finance of a major casino group. He was very clear. He was in the *gaming* business, not the *gambling* business. That is, he wasn't gambling but his customers were, and they *ALWAYS* lose. The proof? The combined casino database of Tahoe, Vegas, and Reno tracks 27 million customers; not one *ever* makes money over the course of a year.)

Here's a simple exercise: take $50 a week to the (pick one) lotto counter, craps table, horse track, blackjack deck, poker room, or bookie. Do this for twenty years. Or, save $50 every week and invest it at compound interest; do this for twenty years. Guess which one has the best chance of making you rich.

"There's an Easier Way"

This section might be summarized as "Financial shortcuts in life almost never pay off." The place those shortcuts take you is down the Path to Poverty. Some things in life, like making and saving money, you just have to work at. Fooling yourself or getting fooled with pipe-dreams and get-rich-quick schemes is another version of the merchandisers' and marketers' snow-jobs discussed in Paths Three and Four – that you deserve or are entitled to some kind of free lunch, some kind of life bonus, because you're special. "The rules don't apply to me." Well, you are special, okay? Just ask your mom. But there are still *no free lunches* when it comes to money.

The professional con artists, human or corporate, who are trying to sell you on the next "sure thing" know your brain better than you do – or at least they did, before you got this book. They know about fear and greed and pleasure, about endorphins and anxiety and agreement, and they know how to bait their traps. When you should be getting alarms from the amygdala (your brain's fear center), with your endorphins running for cover, these silver-tongue hypesters will sweet talk you and stroke your ego until they get their marketing hook sunk hard and deep. Eventually, you'll be flopping on the bank, gasping for air, wondering where your money went. Welcome to the world of the losing proposition, to the enduring truth that "If it sounds too good to be true, it probably is."

Other "losers" are the various forms of cheating, "fixing," bribery, and so on. As you look in the mirror and ask yourself, "Why am I doing this?," also ask, "Is it going to work? Will I get caught? How long will I have to keep it going? Is it serving my goal of security? Is there any long-term satisfaction in it? Do I feel good about myself by doing it? Am I getting rich or living an illusion?" Ask yourself the hard questions. You may not like the answers at first, but you'll realize the risks you're taking and how unreliable these transgressions are.

Pushing the "quick buck, something-for-nothing" angle, in the long-term – ten, twenty years and more – doesn't work. You're stuck with low self-expectations and no real monetary security. You don't grow, you don't get smarter or better at life, you don't get happy. You don't earn respect from yourself or others. And, 98% of the time, you don't get rich.

Isn't He CUTE!

Let's talk about teenagers having babies. "What?" you ask. "How could this possibly fit into a book about personal finance?" Look around. Every young parent out there is nodding his or her head saying, "You bet your booties it does!"

In most cases, teenage pregnancy is a way of taking some kind of shortcut. The girl is trying to get out of her parents' house where she's unhappy, or trying to catch up with her girlfriends who are already mothers, or trying to gratify her own child-bearing instincts before she's got the parenting skills and foundation to raise kids. The boy, if he gets and stays involved, is testing out his own ability to love and his drive to be a provider and a father. Maybe he, too, is trying to escape a family situation, compete with his peers, or meet some other benchmark.

We're not laying down codes of morality here or judging families or people's actions. We're talking *money*. Raising kids is much, *much* more expensive than you'd think. Having them when you're not monetarily prepared is financial quicksand, and most parents will tell you that – even if they did it. You're taking fiscal responsibility for at least one other person's life at a time when you can barely cover your own. When you should be taking classes, studying, or learning a skill to improve your earning potential, you're feeding a baby. When you should be putting $50 in the bank, you can't find $50 for new shoes. When you should be committing yourself more to your new job, you're arguing with your spouse about child care.

Being a teenage parent is a shortcut to twenty years of inescapable hardship, and it's a major obstacle to financial planning. In the worst analysis, you're cheating the child's long-term benefits in pursuit of your own short-term desires. How many kids in America growing up in poverty get a fair shake? In the best analysis, you're burdening everyone with a long, uphill money battle that ought to be planned for a better time. Your reasons for doing it probably don't stand up to an emotional or rational analysis.

Summing Up

Some problems we confront in this chapter – gambling, drugs, loss of schooling, family planning – may need professional advice, even therapy. If so, find help, or contact us on the website and we will point you in the right direction(s). Lots of communities offer peer counseling, often the best and most compassionate source of help. In the bigger picture of life, "security" may mean safety and sanity, not a big bank balance.

However, most of you are now prepared to combat mild versions of these shortcomings through your own grasp on goal-setting, values, power-as-knowledge, and the other lessons in *Paths*. That doesn't mean you can skate; you have to grade yourself from time to time. In the context of this book – money – and especially how it relates to the topics of this chapter, we suggest you do this: settle on your savings goal for the first year, write it down along with your plan of how to get there, start working at it, and then, after three months, pull to the side of the road and check your progress. Are you on track? Are you close? Are you miles short?

If you are falling far short in the first three months, your first concern is with this chapter. The chances are not high that your problem lies here, but you have to go through these topics and rule them out before you go on: Drugs? Gambling? Lack of education? Cheating or other shortcuts? Child worries? These are real-world obstacles to reaching your goals. If you can honestly say these are *not* in your range of problems, anything else, by comparison, is easy to deal with. If you do see where you need to improve, get at it. If you don't, re-read the earlier sections that rung bells for you or, perhaps more important, try to find areas you overlooked or dismissed too easily in the first read, stuff that might hold a key to getting you across the goal line.

EPILOGUE

Is it possible to summarize this book and, perhaps, give an accurate forecast for the future in a few pages? We think so. Why do we even raise this question? Because those two things—a brief but coherent review of the book's arguments and a rational survey for what's over the horizon—will have high value for the reader.

One of the first points we tried to make in *Seven Paths* was the importance of goals to our financial well-being and to life in general. If you want to create beneficial change in your life, you must set goals and learn how to pursue them. We'll drag up another old saying here: "If you don't know where you're going, any road will get you there." That is, if you've got no destination in mind, no intent to create good opportunities and security in your future, then goals aren't important. But if you want a better life in ten years, twenty, and thirty, you must plan for the improvements around a code of written goals. You will need to adjust those goals over time, as situations or priorities change, but you must always have them as a guiding force.

Achieving goals will not by itself bring you happiness. Gordon Livingston, in *Too Soon Old, Too Late Smart,* tells us that happiness comes from good work to do, someone to love, and something to look forward to. Those things revolve around a person's values, so it's essential that your goals be bound to what has real meaning and worth for you. If not, if you build your goals around false values, around artificial views of what's desirable and rewarding, you will spend your blood, sweat, toil, and tears accomplishing things that won't bring you lasting satisfaction, things that can, in fact, bring you poverty.

Our values are based in who we are and who we hope to be. Our ambitions reflect our values and our usefulness to other deserving people and to life in general. Fulfillment of values and achievement of ambitions rely primarily on our ability to maintain and exercise personal power, especially over ourselves and the natural inclinations we all have to take our gratifications today, to take the easy road. The lesson of the Japanese mirror is that learning about yourself, day by day and year by year, gathering information on who you are and how you live your life—these are the keys to controlling your power, to keeping your goals in focus and your life on track. Using your power well is how you will find the most meaning in life and reach the goals that match your values.

It should be obvious now that we don't consider money life's most important element. So why did we write a book about it? Because, good, bad, or ugly, we live in a world in which money plays a critical role in nearly everyone's life and future. As such, it requires a certain amount of attention and planning. Many of the same principles that apply to solving the problems of life also apply to solving the problems of your finances and your monetary future. Goals, values, power, security, planning, selfishness, overindulgence, being thoughtful, being thoughtless, exercise of insight, flexibility, stubbornness, self-deceit, self-esteem, the power of the subconscious—all these factors bear heavily on the ebb and flow of money as well as the management of life. We sincerely hope that what we've written will enhance not only your fiscal stability but your life in the overall.

The "Tour de Finance"

Let's visit the biking-spending analogy a final time to see what it can tell us:

1. Like riding a bike with no hands, some spending for fun is 100% okay. But if you lose control and put your money-bike in the spending ditch every time, you're never going to get to your goal.

2. Buying a flash new bike can just be status seeking, shopping endorphins, or a lack of financial discipline. Buy what you need and will use.

3. You can overdo it. Just as you can over-train on a bike, attack impossible hills, and race before you're ready, making too many financial

sacrifices can kill your motivation. Sometimes sanity comes first.

4. Living on credit is like riding downhill in the dark with your hands off the bars and your eyes closed – fine on a smooth road with no obstacles, but deadly in the real world. And, like lugging extra weight, big interest payments slow you down in saving capital.

"Have We Got a Deal for You!"

We barely entered the investment universe in this book, and that was our intent, which we tried to make clear throughout *Seven Paths*. The scope of that universe is almost infinite, and it requires its own organized exploration. We will "eat that elephant" in our next book, but a few concise comments here should help you.

The "capital markets," as the world of stocks, bonds, insurance, options, banking, venture capitalism, real estate, and business development is sometimes called, form a complex, potentially rewarding, and potentially dangerous arena. "Capital" refers to the money we set loose in these markets in the hope, expectation, assurance, and/or gamble that our capital will make us more capital. Sometimes it doesn't, and sometimes it does. Don't go there without some preparation.

Risk is everywhere—repeat, everywhere. There are all sorts of ways to reduce risk in investing, but it can't be extinguished, and the majority of evidence supports the claim that rewards from investing are proportional to risk. Modest returns should carry modest risk, and high risk should be rewarded with high returns. But this isn't the law, and the problem often is to find the risks you might otherwise miss so that you don't take chances you don't know about and, thereby, either miss returns you should get or get no returns at all.

In large segments of the investment arena, you're playing a "zero-sum game," that is, for every $1000 that one or more investors gain through insight, research, or good luck, one or more investors lose the same amount through lack of insight, faulty research, or bad luck. And often, it seems, the luck factor trumps the other two. But study and experience, which we intend to deliver in *Seven Doors,* combined with patience, which you must deliver, can usually put the odds more in your favor.

Some investments are geared toward development – that is, taking the raw material of natural resources, land, revolutionary ideas or technologies, business concepts, and the like and turning them into enterprises that perform an economic or other practical function. This should not be a zero-sum game. In a properly executed development, the resulting sum should be more than the cost of the parts that went in to creating it, i.e. money, brains, and materials. This isn't to say all "development" has high social or human value—some does and some doesn't. You must decide what enterprises you want to support by investing in them.

There are other investments, like bonds and T-bills, that are simply loans by other names. You provide capital, are paid a consistent specified interest rate for a nominated period, then get your capital back in the same dollar amount you put it in. Modest reward. It should carry modest, conservative risk. Be sure it does.

We believe that investing requires a lot of study and a lot of effort. If it was easy to make a ton of money investing over the short term, do you know what? Everyone would be doing it, and everyone would be rich. But they're not. In fact, some people who invest do it badly and end up with little benefit to show for it years later. (These people usually display some combination of Paths Four, Five, and Seven.) The truth is that investing is often unsafe, unpredictably risky, deceptively complex, and frequented by charlatans, good-time Charlies and Charlenes, and people who are replete with the flaws of the *Seven Paths,* often in triplicate. So, we believe that young investors need to make all the prudent preparation they can. As Mr. Charles Libbey says, "Proper prior planning prevents piss-poor performance." To that end, we ask you to look for *The Seven Golden Doors* at your favorite bookstore or website, and if you don't find it, go to *our* website.

Our Crystal Ball

What will the future bring? More of the same, and things we've never seen before. That is, basic human nature is not going to change, but the things people do and how they do them *will* change, and those changes will come faster and more dramatically in your future than you could ever conceive of today. The flaws and strengths of the human condition that history has taught us will always be there. The innocence and green pride of youth, the expanding talents of young adults finding their power, the harmonious productivity of dedicated experts working together to produce great things, the wisdom and contributions of mature people who mean to leave the world a better place than they found it— these will all be churning until the world that we know is gone. Regrettably, also, we will see the sins, the crimes, the failures, and the injuries caused by those who learn nothing from history, or too much.

Just as true, you must look forward to change, to anticipate it. It will always come. Much of it you will welcome, some of it you will reject, and some of it you will dread. But don't fear change. The fact is, with clear goals and your own power, you can change your life, and you can change the world. One of the classics in this area is *Futureshock,* by Alvin Toffler. (*F/S* is part of his trilogy, as is *Powershift,* which we mentioned earlier.) It's not a great book just because of what it predicts, but also in how it chronicles history. It "calibrates the clock of change," so to speak, detailing the light-speed at which transitions are made. (Inside every older person is a younger person asking himself, "What just happened?")

Again, finance imitates life: it's full of change and full of the unchanged. Politicians' faces are still on the money, thirty pieces of silver can still buy betrayal, the money-changers are still in the temple, and you still should plan for a rainy day—or *forty*. But now you can move mountains of dollars with a computer, buy property in Malta over the phone, and change Chinese yuan into Chilean pesos with an email. Opportunities are everywhere, but they work both ways. Use caution. Be prudent.

Live It Up!

None of this book is worth the keyboard it was written on if it doesn't help you have a better life, and some of that is having fun. Ride bikes. Read books. Hike in Patagonia. Go the Tate Modern. Have a drink. Ski in Andorra. Go to grad school to study what you love. Explore the Kelabit highlands in Borneo. Have more kids than some people think is wise. Throw flowers at a parade. Pick nectarines in New Zealand. Pray with your eyes open. Barbecue on the beach. Make wine. Pet dogs. Cook good food. Love your lover(s). Love your friend(s). Go to town. Give gifts. Float on your back. Catch fish.

But realize there's a future you'll have to meet. Accept your responsibilities. Use conscious thought. Develop a love for work—some kind of work. Save some money every week. Learn about investing. Be safe. Give credit and respect to those who gave you your shot at life. Be trustworthy. Trust those who have earned your trust. Protect your welfare, including the security around which this book revolves. And remember something a friend told us as we were writing this book: If you buy everything you want when you're young, you can't afford what you need when you're old, but if you only buy what you need when you're young, you can afford anything you want when you're old.

FROM THE COAL-FACE

The term "coal-face" refers to the section deep in the mine where the real work gets done, where the valuable product—coal—gets separated from the rock and the dirt. We thought a few interviews with some professional "diggers," people who have dealt with thousands of clients' financial affairs, would provide some additional depth and color to *Seven Paths*.

JA is a senior accounts manager at a local accountancy firm. MM is a tax analyst who oversees preparation of returns from the most complex to simple 1040s for a national tax consultancy and preparation service. RW was the founder of a local commercial bank and owns a property management and real-estate operations firm that services nearly 2500 rental units covering more than 100 miles of California coast. The combined experience of these three specialists exceeds 100 years.

JA interview
7P: Because you're a mother to young women and you also handle important financial transactions for your

firm's clients, we'd like to hear some of your experiences with how people handle their money.

Do you see any links between how young people handle their finances and how their families do?

JA: Without a doubt, but it's not as automatic as it might seem. Some people mimic their parents, and some do the opposite. Depression-era parents with frugal values might serve as examples for their kids, or they might cause their kids to rebel and go in the other direction, with no-holds-barred spending. In this community you see all the extremes as well as the middle road. But what ever patterns you see, individual behavior always reflects family behavior—or its opposite.

I'm an example. My parents were children of the Depression, very careful with money, and I have a free-spending streak that I keep under control, with some success. I have an internal dialogue about it all the time. One of my daughters has had some difficult times keeping her financial life together, but seems on top of it now. The other one caught on quicker and now, at age twenty-five, is a home owner.

7P: Give us two or three examples of money mismanagement you've seen that led young adults into financial hardship.

JA: Cars. Clothes. Cell phones. All the goo.

7P: The *goo?*

JA: Yes, the goo, the image props. We deal with young entrepreneurs, self-made successes, get-rich wannabes, trust-fund accounts, misguided investors, professionals, mom-and-pops—all sorts. It's easy to compare them.

The ones who feel compelled to put the appearance of success—all the goo—ahead of an actual and stable profit stream always get in trouble. All the show of status in the world won't take the place of a commitment to hard work and understanding your business.

We had an abalone diver who thought he just had to drive a Mercedes sedan because the guy who ran the seafood export market in Los Angeles did. He was a good, successful diver and knew the business, but he thought he had to show all the trappings of a wealth he didn't have when he rubbed shoulders with other people in the business. It went from the car to high-end hospitality parties to lavish gifts for business contacts, all from an income stream that just didn't justify it. You can't take an image to the bank.

7P: Do you have any examples of your clients showing successful or healthy patterns in how they handle money?

JA: Making a good business plan and sticking with it. Setting goals and putting those goals in first priority when it comes to the finances of their businesses. Not spending up large just because the books look good for a few months or even a couple of years. Or because you've convinced yourself they will look good somewhere down the road. Financial success in business has a long time horizon. Invest in your business first.

7P: Over the years that you've managed finances for clients and your firm, what damaging changes have you seen regarding young adults and their access to and use of money? What healthy changes?

JA: Credit cards can lead to crippling debt. Credit cards plus "the goo" can paint a pretty ugly financial picture in a short time if the profits decide not to tango with the expectations. Your accountant and bookkeeper are there for good reasons, not just to deal with Uncle Sam. Get their advice and use it when it comes to financial planning.

7P: Give us any other information you can about how people successfully handle their money, or don't.

JA: I'll take the "or don't" option first. Let's go back to cars, because they're a big-ticket item, have a lot of caché in our culture, and buying them can be full of tricks. Flash cars don't pay the bills, add to your investment fund, pay your employees, and so forth. Neither do the Prada wardrobe nor the Caribbean vacations. These things should only appear when the business plan is on track.

7P: Any savings or investment advice for young people as they move out into the world?

JA: Start yesterday.

MM interview

7P: Because you've been working with the tax records of thousands of people for over thirty-two years, you have seen a lot of colorful and educational examples of people and money. We'd like to record some of the lessons you've seen at work in the tax world.

Of the people you serve over fifty, what percentage of them show signs of being on track for a financially secure retirement, outside of Social Security or an employment pension?

MM: Perhaps 10%. In communities with low costs of living, married couples who have paid off their homes and have modest spending habits can squeak by on two-person Social Security payments and some modest savings.   But if they have an ongoing mortgage, indulgent spending, or live in a higher-cost community, they will really struggle without some savings and investments.

7P: Of those who appear headed for financial independence, do you see any patterns in how they achieved it?   Savings?   Investment success?   Tax planning?

MM: Unfortunately, we don't see enough people who do good tax planning. That would help a lot of them. The ones we see in good financial position for retirement started saving and investing early, have self-discipline, and had a lot of stability – in their jobs and their family situations.

7P: Do you see any people under thirty-five who show signs of good retirement planning?

MM: Yes and no, and they're all over the map. Again, stability and starting early are the two big factors. If they take part in their employers' retirement plan options, and leave that money invested and untouched, they do much better. But the ones who spend all they earn or don't have an eye on the future – they'll be in trouble.

7P: Two or three examples of unwise or dangerous patterns?

MM: Same arguments of instability and not starting early. We see young people changing jobs frequently and liquidating their 401Ks, and so on, from each job. They seem to say, "Oh, that's not much money. It won't really make a difference." So they cash it out, pay the tax, and spend the money.

7P: They can't see the future dollar value?

MM: Exactly right. A person might do this three or four times, liquidate a few thousand each time. Call it $12,000 total. Invested carefully over twenty years, that could be worth well over $100,000. Instead, they pay 40% out in tax and spend the rest. They don't understand that they're undermining their own futures.

7P: Do you see general patterns with people who seem obviously headed for poverty and hardship after sixty?

MM: The old story of living beyond their means, carrying high debt into retirement, and so forth.

7P: If you could give young people two pieces of advice – one on savings and one on investments – what would they be?

MM: Pay attention – to your savings, your investments, and your spending. No one will look after your financial welfare as well as you will.

RW Interview

7P: Because of your experience in the banking world, and because you've worked with college student housing for eighteen-to-twenty-five-year-olds for forty years, we'd like to get your opinions and ideas about how young people handle money. Do you see any links between parents and children in the handling of finances?

RW: A few comments first. In recent years we've seen a marked trend of young adults to be more dependent on their parents. Parents are more involved in their children's daily lives on almost every level at ages when young adults could be showing much more authority and responsibility. We see more young people incapable of managing their daily lives.

This extended dependency causes a lack of real-world money experience as basic as buying food and paying bills. College students eighteen to twenty-one years old drive cars worth $20,000 to $30,000 and more, spend their rent money on parties and entertainment, but can't balance a checkbook or live within their means. Flagrant dishonesty and deception aren't common, but they usually reflect family traits. The apple doesn't fall far from the tree. People sloppy in their manners, their studies, and their finances tend to be sloppy in their thinking, and vice-versa. Lack of financial competence follows the same patterns.

7P: Give us some examples of money mismanagement you've seen that led young adults into financial hardship.

RW: Spending without boundaries on toys and entertainment. Open access to money with few enforced rules and limits encourages free spending. Credit cards, cell phones, the Internet, and the rest give kids access to under-controlled spending power. Some lose their way. This leads to all the down-stream financial problems: credit card debt, unpaid bills, bad credit, and then all the dramatic increases in costs that can bring: higher bank fees, lending fees, and interest rates, higher rents and deposits.

7P: Do you have any examples of your young clients showing successful or healthy patterns in how they handle money?

RW: The low-key kids, the ones who work side jobs and vacation jobs, who earn their own money or are funded with clear guidelines and responsibility learn money reality early, the benefits of secure finance, and how quickly it can escape if it is ignored.

7P: Over the thirty years you've managed property for college students, what damaging changes have you seen regarding young adults and their access to and use of money? What healthy changes?

RW: The consumer-market orientation of kids is very strong and creates a sinkhole for money. This psychology plus a large allowance turns wants and desires into needs, and too often there's no one there to rein in behavior. But some kids are capable of rising above that. They pay the bills, spend on essentials as well as some fun stuff, but seem to have internal limits: self-imposed values and rules on what money is for at this stage of their lives, how to use it, and that it's limited. This, also, comes from parental influence.

7P: Give us any other information you can about how people successfully handle their money, or don't.

RW: It's an all-day discussion, but I think we've covered what we see that's most disruptive to monetary security. We see too much abuse of landlords' property. This goes hand-in-hand with disrespect for others, and this breeds bad behavior and a life-long selfish outlook. These trends lead to legal actions, evictions, lawsuits, and all of these can create huge financial distress for the guilty parties.

7P: Any savings or investment advice for these people as they move out into the world?

RW: Present versus future value of money, and how small amounts today create big amounts tomorrow, is critical information. You've told me that this is a major theme in your book, and it can't be overemphasized.

Credit misuse is extremely expensive. Banks make significant money with service fees, late charges, NSF fees, and so forth.

If an item is needed or desired, better to save until you can purchase something of quality that will last versus something that may need to be replaced in the short-term.

Acknowledgements

We'd like to express our sincere gratitude to those who have helped us take this project from a very rough jumble of words and ideas to a product we're proud to present to the reading public. We attribute much of the strength of the material and its structure to these people; we accept all errors and omissions as our own.

Our heartfelt thanks go out to: the Byrne family: Norma, Silas, Lauren (Ryan), Tristan, Michael and Dottie (Larson), and to Sharon Bifano, Don and Di Flanigan, and Art and Marsha Gossard. We would not be in print without our editor Katherine McCracken, our publishing advisor Robert Tucker, and knight protector Mike Pfau. We want to voice our appreciation to the following for their valuable time in reading our early drafts and giving us invaluable guidance on concepts neglected, prejudices favored, and/or phrasing overdone: Douglas Ades, Bill and Margie Campbell, Richard McKenzie, Ed McKinley, Robin McPhail, Ron Mittino, Larry Nelson, Bill Paulin, Mike Pfau, Jeffrey Skinner, Jeff Sloane, and Barry Spacks.

We want to thank Bob Fulmer for his time, encouragement, and lessons from personal experience, and the three professionals in the preceding section who asked to remain unnamed.

Finally, Gary and Lance want to express the debts we owe to the WLPA – you know who you are – with a special thanks to Jørgen Kjaempe.